D1466714

Momentum

Momentum

How Companies Become Unstoppable Market Forces

Ron Ricci

John Volkmann

HARVARD BUSINESS SCHOOL PRESS

BOSTON, MASSACHUSETTS

Printed in the United States of America

07 06 05 04 03   5 4 3 2 1

Requests for permission to use or reproduce material from
this book should be directed to permissions@hbsp.harvard.edu,
or mailed to Permissions, Harvard Business School Publishing,
60 Harvard Way, Boston, Massachusetts 02163.

Library of Congress Cataloging-in-Publication Data

Ricci, Ron.
    Momentum : how companies become unstoppable market forces /
Ron Ricci, John Volkmann.
       p. cm.
    Includes bibliographical references and index.
    ISBN 1-57851-522-X (alk. paper)
      1. Marketing—Technological innovations.   2. Internet marketing.
    3. Brand name products—Marketing.   4. Strategic planning.
    I. Volkmann, John.   II. Title.
       HF5415 .R5416 2002
       658.8'27—dc21

                                                    2002007487

The paper used in this publication meets the requirements of the
American National Standard for Permanence of Paper for Publications
and Documents in Libraries and Archives Z39.48-1992.

To
Loretta, Annie, and Jake Ricci
and
Denise, Ryan, Danielle, and Rachel Volkmann

Our own sources of momentum

Contents

Acknowledgments

SO MANY PEOPLE helped us to produce this book. We would like to thank the following people:

Andrea "Andy" Cunningham of Citigate Cunningham for letting us pursue our dream of understanding why some of the greatest brands of our generation were losing in the marketplace. She and the board of Citigate Cunningham made the five-year commitment to see our work through to completion. In our decade together at Cunningham Communication, she provided the working conditions in which we were able to recognize, explore, and cultivate the ideas discussed in this book.

Richard Smith at Sprint and Keith Fox and Bob Michelet at Cisco for taking the chance on our research proposals and conceptual models when they were little more than ideas on PowerPoint slides.

Acknowledgments

Bill MacElroy of Socratic Research for shepherding us through the research model that validated our ideas about momentum.

Jay Shutter and his brilliant team at the Momentum Research Group for honing our momentum research model into the marketing dashboard that we hope will help companies manage their market positions more effectively.

The many Citigate Cunningham coworkers who contributed to this work, including Tein Atkerson, Frank Bailinson, Morris Denton, Sue Earabino, Andy Elder, Joe Hamilton, Jeremy Hartman, Carrie Mancini, Meghan O'Leary, Rich Phillips, Andy Steen, Lynne Waldera, Peggy Wood, and many others.

Tom Parker for his invaluable help in crafting the book proposal that introduced us to Sandy Dijkstra, our agent, who in turn introduced us to Kirsten Sandberg, our editor at Harvard Business School Press, who always had a sense of clarity about what needed to be done to make this work better.

John Chambers for generously giving us access to his insights and all of Cisco's market experiences—and, ultimately, a job.

The many Cisco coworkers who helped in the process of writing this book, including Maureen Kasper, Dan Scheinman, Donna Soave, and Rochelle Steele.

Bruce Chizen of Adobe, Rob Glaser of Real Networks, Joe Nacchio of Qwest, Craig Conway of PeopleSoft, and the other CEOs who bought into and then invested in thought leadership–based executive marketing platforms. Nacchio also helped us understand the necessity of looking at momentum as a marketing vocabulary for executives unfamiliar with the digital product model.

Don Listwin of OpenWave for helping us to imagine the possibilities of combining the six forces of differentiation in multiple ways as strategies to sustain differentiation over time.

The many clients—Lorene Arey, Jack Browne, Elaine Chang, Melissa Drydahl, Murray Goldman, Mike Gullard, Linda Hayes, Dave Larson, Michael Marks, Rod McGeary, Bob Priest-Heck, Hector Ruiz, Joyce Strand, Jim Zemlin, and so many more—who indulged us as consultants and confidants.

And finally, our families—Loretta, Annie, and Jake Ricci and Denise, Ryan, Danielle, and Rachel Volkmann—for their patience with us late at night, on weekends, on vacations, and whenever else we could find time to research, think, and write.

Momentum

Introduction

THIS BOOK EXAMINES the interrelationships among product strategy, brand, and a market's value chain structure, and the impact of digital technologies on these relationships. Throughout this book, we describe a model for a *momentum*-based business strategy as a form of strategic positioning for companies that compete for customers who are used to the peculiarities of digital technologies. To express how customers choose and remain loyal to digital products and services, we introduce *brand momentum* both as the conceptual framework to capture the mind-set of digital customers, and as a marketing dashboard to manage differentiation and loyalty in the context of the expectations people have for digital offerings over the course of a product's life cycle.

Since positioning has many connotations, we've adopted Michael Porter's definition to describe our own work: "Strategic positioning means performing *different* activities from rivals' or performing similar activities in *different ways*."[1] It was clear from our consulting experiences working with Motorola, IBM, Kodak, and Hewlett-Packard in the early to mid-1990s that Intel, EMC, Microsoft, and Sun Microsystems were harnessing a new set of market forces in new or different ways from our clients. These new leaders were consistently gaining share and building superior market value, yet it was difficult to convince senior management at Kodak, et al. to recognize and act on the new forces influencing differentiation as it existed in the eyes of the beholders who mattered most: customers. The models we introduce in this book to help companies manage their differentiation with customers are the end result of primary research that includes more than 20,000 customer interviews. We discuss the framework for this research in chapters 1 and 2.

The success of Intel, EMC, Microsoft, and Sun demonstrated that a dominant market position no longer guaranteed a continued market advantage. Consider that Colgate toothpaste lost its market share advantage over Crest in 1962. It wasn't until Colgate introduced the Total toothpaste product and brand strategy more than thirty-five years later that Colgate finally created enough differentiation to regain the market's top position. Coke has held its market share lead over Pepsi—forever—despite a major product miss ("New Coke") and anxious moments in advertising when Ray Charles and the "Pepsi Generation" had Coca-Cola scrambling for younger customers. The same is true for Kodak film; while Fuji has slowly eroded Kodak's leadership position, the famous yellow box remains the top seller in the United States by about fifty share points. And despite years of stagnant car brands, General Motors is still the largest carmaker in the United States. GM lost market share in thirteen of the fourteen years between 1987 and 2001, yet the carmaker maintained its lead over Ford by a few share points. On the other hand, Intel, EMC, Microsoft, Sun, and many other companies we discuss later captured top market share positions in dramatically shorter cycles and subsequently fought back leadership challenges every couple of years from the digital equivalents of Colgate's Total. Yet these four companies created more than $650 billion total in market value as of the end of 2001, even after the dramatic decline in stock market values over the previous two years.

In the summer of 1996, we set out to discover precisely why and how these new market forces worked, and what impact these changes had on how people perceived the brands they bought. Many of the fundamental observations about digital technologies that we describe and apply in this book were incubated in the personal computer industry and later exported to other digital markets. If any single factor seemed to characterize the PC business, as well as other digital markets, including cell phones, pagers, and video game machines—not to mention the massive, $1 trillion-a-year global information technology and telecommunications markets—it was the sense of constant motion around any product category. Products never seemed to move in any absolute direction for more than four or five years. And it wasn't just the pace of technological advancement; the rapid evolution of value points, such as chips, operating systems, applications software, networking, servers, printers, storage, video game platforms, and many others, brought swarms of companies and venture capital dollars into the market. As a result, the sense of motion surrounding digital products possesses a kind of kinetic energy. Digital markets seem to work like a wind tunnel, in which the wind speed constantly accelerates while waves of different flying objects invade the tunnel to rearrange the conditions for survival.

The static nature of markets like toothpaste, film, cars, and airplanes, among thousands of others, produced approaches to strategic positioning that would never be completely appropriate for digital products and services. It took us a while to make the initial connection, but we ultimately settled on physics as the fundamental conceptual underpinning of the models we present in this book. Digital markets are intrinsically dynamic, and momentum comes straight from the field of mechanics and the study of dynamic conditions. So you could say Newton pointed the way. From observation and experience, certain companies in every digital market have leveraged a combination of product strategy, brand, and the unique structure of a particular market's value chain to become unstoppable *forces* in the minds of customers, with nearly unassailable market positions.

But we knew that to effectively explain the unique nature of differentiation as it exists in digital markets, we would need more than a clever theory based on physics. Physicist Stephen Hawking says that all good theories have two characteristics: They explain a large field of observations, and they are able to predict future observations. That is precisely the goal of this book: to use our model to help companies harness the market forces unique to digital markets to build and sustain differentiated positions with customers.

But it was 1996, and we had a long way to go. Time was of the essence. We had already witnessed wild market valuation swings in which a company's value ballooned or shrank by billions of dollars over shorter and shorter spans of time. Sometimes it also appeared that billions moved from one company's market cap to another's, often in periods of a month or less. At the time, most industry watchers were predicting that the Internet would further accelerate this phenomenon and change the forces of differentiation even more dramatically.

As we started our journey, we recalled an old proverb a friend of ours from Kodak quoted frequently: "Draw your friends close, but your enemies closer." Instead of setting out to understand what *wasn't* working for our heavyweight clients, we decided to increase our understanding of what *was* working for the new winners.

In the end, our inquiry yielded a simple, if unexpected, clue: Larry Ellison.

I

Why Momentum?

IN 1996, ORACLE collaborated with Sun, IBM, and Netscape on a technical specification for a new kind of computer, the network computer, or NC. Oracle's founder and CEO, Larry Ellison, offered a vision of computing as a utility—not unlike electricity—that could be easily accessed via the inexpensive, appliance-like NC. In Oracle's 1997 annual report, Ellison wrote:

> *It's impossible for me to write a letter or make a speech without mentioning the Network Computer or NC. The NC idea is simple and the need is clear: there will be no information age until computers are as easy to use as telephones, and as inexpensive as televisions.*[1]

At the core of the NC's positioning, as Ellison pointed out in the many speeches he would give to evangelize the NC, was a direct challenge to Microsoft's domination of the software industry at a time when Netscape and the Internet were planting seeds that Microsoft was vulnerable. Ellison had very practical reasons to suggest that Microsoft had a soft underbelly: Microsoft threatened Oracle's strategic position in databases, the product category underlying Oracle's relationship with customers and the source of the company's market value with Wall Street.

The NC wasn't the first time Ellison created news and piqued customer interest by providing a compelling context for, and putting a human face on, a confluence of market forces. In 1994, Oracle hosted a press conference at CBS Studios in Los Angeles. Ellison was making news again, this time with the venerable Walter Cronkite at his side. In a cavernous television studio, surrounded by a complete mock–living room set, Ellison touted what he called a "media server," which would make interactive television possible, delivering movies on demand to subscribers—not just the handful of movies available on a cable system's pay-per-view channels, but any movie people wanted to see, any time they wanted to see it. In Ellison's vision, movies-on-demand was the ultimate application of client-server computing—the very same approach to computing that was emerging as the successor to IBM mainframes in the data centers of the largest companies around the world. For a few months, the media server and the NC each spawned press frenzies, as Oracle organized campaigns to influence market gurus and opinion leaders—the people we on the inside of the technology industry refer to as the "influencers of the influencers." This attention was followed by timely investments in the concepts, especially the NC, from venture and equity markets and by a string of deals between the biggest names in consumer electronics and information technology.

The personal passion, market insight, and hyperbole of Ellison's view of the opportunities created by the media server and the NC gave them a "bet-the-company" feel. It wasn't Oracle's New Coke—when Coca-Cola risked the Coke brand franchise with a new, sweeter formula—but any significant reward always comes with the risk of failure and the consequences of failure for a company's strategic position with customers. In Oracle's case, the exact opposite happened. In almost the same time it took for the media server and NC to look like promising product and market opportunities, Oracle's core customers rejected the concepts, and the viability of the media server and the NC collapsed. Yet Oracle's market share with customers went *up* for five consecutive years after the launch of the NC, and Oracle ultimately captured two-thirds of the market for database products based on UNIX, the preferred operating system for client-server applications and, later, for many Internet-based applications.

In some important way, the media server and the NC succeeded in building customers' belief that Oracle was the right choice for them, even as their strategic technology choices were still evolving in the post–IBM computing world. Ironically, the demise of the media server and the NC validated Oracle's position in customers' minds as the company with the product strategy most likely to overcome whatever future challenges might be required of database technology—the exact predicament these same customers hoped to *avoid* by choosing Oracle. During this time, Microsoft also contributed to Oracle's success, as our research would later identify. Microsoft's handling of the U.S. Department of Justice's antitrust investigation of its business practices and a number of other high-profile industry issues established Microsoft's own corporate integrity as a greater threat to its market position with customers than competitive offerings. We will discuss this research and its implications for Microsoft in chapter 5.

Clearly Ellison understood how to draw attention to himself and his company by moving beyond simple product announcements. Ellison did two things particularly well in his role as industry visionary. First, he aligned the underlying technology trends of the information technology industry and positioned them as powerful market forces made up of products and companies with a common enemy: Microsoft. Second, he personalized the concepts in ways virtually anyone could understand. In this way, he intuitively grasped, before many of his contemporaries did, that customers would ultimately reward him for taking risks—even when his big ideas failed. In looking back on our experiences with EMC, Intel, Sun, and Microsoft, we found that similar issues existed for each company; each featured a CEO with a visionary agenda whose public persona was larger than life, especially when compared to our clients who were losing market share—IBM's John Akers, Motorola's Gary Tooker, Hewlett-Packard's Lew Platt, and Kodak's Kay Whitmore.

As we began the discovery phase of our research, in which we hoped to establish the conceptual framework for our planned quantitative research, we wanted to better understand how Ellison's future view of the media server and the NC contributed to the company's aura of differentiation, and how they reflected on Oracle's core products. We had witnessed similar combinations of factors at work with EMC's Michael

Ruettgers, Intel's Andy Grove, Sun's Scott McNealy, and Microsoft's Bill Gates, and we wondered, Is a compelling market vision linked to a product strategy and a charismatic personality enough to create genuine differentiation with customers? We used this question to start our inquiry into how customers—people—perceive differentiation in the context of digital technologies and what consequence these perceptions have on loyalty over the course of a customer relationship.

DIFFERENTIATION—FROM THE DIGITAL PERSPECTIVE

We began by auditing consulting assignments we had done with Fortune 500 companies, hot start-ups, and typical Silicon Valley market challengers. One of these assignments involved pages and pages of transcribed qualitative interviews with CIOs and other top technology decision makers from businesses in the process of making large, million-dollar database purchases. The interviews had been conducted by an advertising agency on behalf of a high-flying database company that we'd been hired to position in its ongoing market struggle with Oracle. As we pored over these transcripts at the ad agency's Palo Alto offices, we came across a line that would resonate for us throughout the transcript review. "Well," one customer said, "Oracle just seems ... *inevitable*."

It turned out that in many of the interviews, respondents referred, either directly or indirectly, to their belief in the *inevitability* of Oracle's success in the database market as a key factor in their decision making. Incredibly, this belief existed despite customers' own acknowledged views of Oracle as having a poor customer-satisfaction track record and a generally acknowledged follower position in technology. Yet Oracle seemed unstoppable in customers' minds. As evidence of Oracle's "inevitability," customers noted Ellison's appearances in the media, with partners, at industry conferences, and on Wall Street, in which he talked about his vision for the media server and the NC. Larry Ellison, the person, was clearly embedded in the Oracle brand as a core element of the company's differentiation.

From our point of view, we were observing what brand gurus such as David Aaker, David Ogilvy, and Trout and Ries predicted for decades: Purchase and loyalty are empirically linked to how people *perceive* differentiation. But differentiation, whether real or fabricated, exists only in the context of a person's expectations for a product or service. We were certain that two decades of using PCs, software, servers, cell phones, pagers, video games, personal digital assistants (PDAs), and, of course, the Internet—among the panoply of digital products and services pervading our lives today—had influenced people's expectations for products. The sense of inevitability described by Oracle's customers appealed to us because it suggested a state of mind for the digital customer, rather than an attribute such as customer service. We decided at this point to attempt to model the purchase considerations that created this state of mind, as well as how those considerations influenced the sources of differentiation valued most by people when purchasing a digital product or service.

What's on People's Minds?

As the process for understanding these purchase considerations, we examined the general market experiences of leaders inside and outside technology markets, including companies such as GE, Cisco, Gillette, Merck, Charles Schwab, and Lexus. We also tried to understand the failure to hold market share leadership by looking at Apple (circa 1996), Cadillac, Memorex, Atari, and other companies that had fallen from grace or hadn't achieved much to begin with. Often we compared companies from completely different industries to see if the comparisons provided insights into the mind-set of the digital customer. In this process, two contrasting case studies stood out from the others in helping us to understand the purchase decision-making process every digital customer goes through, and the reason people's expectations for differentiation had fundamentally evolved, or were in the process of doing so.

1. *Digital products are never finished.* Consider the difference between buying a car, say, an Acura, and a PDA like the PalmPilot. The Acura follows a traditional consumption pattern. It is purchased or leased, driven for a number of years, serviced or repaired as necessary, and then replaced. The essential elements of the car—the engine and the chassis—remain with the vehicle after the owner sells it. Memories, as well as nonessential items like add-on cup holders or music CDs, are the only aspects of the car that a person carries forward from one vehicle to another. In contrast, anyone buying a Palm sees today's unit as merely a temporary home for its most essential application—the ability to manage dates and addresses. The buyer knows the basic functionality of the product category is changing

quickly; tomorrow's products will be better in some way than today's. The consumption pattern is the exact opposite of the Acura. Rather than memories or impressions, people carry forward the most important aspect of what they are actually doing from one product to another—in the case of the Palm, the address and calendar information. Memories of using the old device matter only if the experience of using the latest device fails to live up to the previous Palm. The fundamental difference can best be described as the distinction between marketing the past and marketing the future. (However, more than a dozen major car brands now offer General Motors's OnStar services for select cars, potentially elevating the role of digital technologies in the purchase consideration of an automobile. With two million subscribers and a history of ten million individual customer experiences with its services, OnStar is introducing Palm-like considerations into the car buying experience. The plethora of OnStar's value-add driving services, from safety and security information to online diagnostics, is introducing personalized information that people may expect to carry forward with them when they upgrade their car, just like they do with a Palm. While On-Star is not the primary purchase consideration for a car—yet—its subscriber base increased by 250 percent in 2001, and it will be interesting to see how subscribers react the next time they purchase a car if the service *isn't* available. In other mass markets, companies like Sears, Panasonic, General Electric, and Sony are exploring digital services comparable to OnStar for entertainment products and household goods such as refrigerators and microwave ovens. As these services mature, we expect that the momentum strategies we discuss in the following chapters will apply to these markets even when the product's primary function is analog-powered, but the customer relationship is digital-centric. Over the horizon, GM is experimenting with a concept car called AUTOnomy, which envisions a Dell-like approach to building cars based on a common, scalable technology platform. It is not quite a Windows-based PC, but AUTOnomy and the many other "white-board" concepts in corporate research labs around the world are fundamentally enabled by digital technologies and

will certainly introduce considerations particular to those technologies at some point in
the future.)

2. *Digital products never stand alone.* When we
compared Sun's Java software technology to
Gillette's Mach3 razor, it became clear that
our model also had to accommodate a second
peculiarity specific to the digital product
model. Consider the difference between these
two technology and market share leaders.
Gillette has maintained a 60 percent to 70 percent share of the razor market since the 1960s
by introducing a new blade design every
decade or so. The Mach3 razor continued this
tradition with a new and innovative blade
configuration. A conventional, stand-alone
product, the Mach3 works on virtually any
beard and with every kind of shaving cream. It
is in Gillette's best interest, then, to keep the
Mach3 technology proprietary and to build a
distinct brand position for this razor that re-
tains as much of its value proposition for
Gillette, and Gillette alone, as possible. In contrast, Java technology established Sun as a software leader on a scale that for several years
threatened Microsoft. But before the company

could leverage Java as a differentiator, Sun had to give Java away for virtually nothing to its fiercest competitors, some of whom were many times Sun's size with far greater customer clout. In Sun's market—and in virtually every digital product category—products never stand alone. Every customer application of the digital technology is actually a collection of interdependent products working together to function and add value in some particular way. Java only had value as a differentiator for Sun if it became a marketplace opportunity for hundreds, if not thousands, of other companies selling something based on Java, not just an opportunity exclusive to Sun. Thus, it was in Sun's best interest to diffuse the promise of Java to as many companies as possible.

Back to the Future

After reviewing these case studies and others, we decided to more precisely understand how these two peculiar considerations of digital technologies influenced the way people form opinions when purchasing digital products and services. We looked back in time to better understand the differences between buying an "analog" product like shaving cream or a car and a digital product like the Palm or Java. We started with the early Apple computers in the late 1970s, the precursors to many of today's mass-market digital products, and we quickly realized that it was too simplistic to think of products as simply "digital," as too much had changed so quickly since 24 kilobytes of computer memory was considered a lot. Over the past twenty-five years, the unique purchase considerations intrinsic to all digital products have not changed, in our observation; if anything, the underlying pace of these factors has increased. The sophistication of the people buying the products, on the other hand, has changed dramatically with the increasingly deeper penetration of digital products and services inside corporations and into our lifestyles. We think that during this time the digital mind-set evolved in three stages. Each of the three stages covered over the next few pages helped us to better understand how purchase consideration, expectations, and differentiation evolved as people's experiences with digital products evolved.

- *Stage I, the Marketplace of Image,* was born out of the modern marketing revolution of the 1960s. At the time of the introduction of the Apple I and Apple II, the dominant approach to creating and managing differentiation for business and consumer audiences was based on brand image and brand equity. The Marketplace of Image focused on creating differentiation by marketing the *past* to customers. Successful brands emphasized customers' existing positive associations with a product as a reason to buy more. "People don't buy products, they buy brands" was a key axiom. We'll point out shortly why image is not exactly everything when it comes to digital products and services. However, the role of image as a symbol of trust and integrity remains vital to any consistently successful product or service—digital or otherwise.

- *Stage II, the Marketplace of Products,* emerged in the 1980s and early 1990s as a phenomenon driven by the mass-market potential of digital products and services. The Marketplace of Products focused on marketing the *present* to customers. Companies used product features to gain and regain customer loyalty.

- *Stage III, the Marketplace of Ideas,* evolved in the late 1990s and at the turn of the century out of the unique purchase considerations of digital technologies and the emergence of digital products as business, cultural, and lifestyle forces. This stage casts an expansive look into the *future.*

THE MARKETPLACE OF IMAGE

The fundamental principles of differentiation in the Marketplace of Image were constructed for products that were slow to evolve, relatively low-tech, and more alike than unalike. Marketers aspiring to build a differentiated position with customers faced the challenge of creating differentiation where little existed.

As a result, branding emerged as a form of strategic positioning. Brands started as an amalgam of symbols and impressions—many having little if anything to do with the products themselves—conveyed to customers. Branding focused instead on tapping into images and emotions, especially focusing on customers' early experiences with the brand. Instead of simply buying products, consumers bought into the *image* that marketers were able to create around those products. Rather than buy a cola drink, for example, customers were urged to seek admission to the ever-youthful "Pepsi Generation"; rather than buy a pack of cigarettes, customers purchased a ticket (one-way, for many) to "Marlboro Country."

The most valuable and durable brands, such as Kodak, Coca-Cola, Sony, and many others, have translated what consumers *believe* about their brands into a sustainable image for decades. The strength of these associations allowed Kodak, Coca-Cola, and Sony to maintain their existing customer bases while also attracting new customers and consistently building equity, or value, in the brand image.

The brand equity model, developed in the 1970s and 1980s, established a way to qualify and quantify the value of a person's past experiences with a brand. Brand scholar David Aaker suggests these past experiences could be measured in four ways: through brand awareness, brand associations, brand loyalty, and perceived quality.

Brand equity is credited with placing a dollar value on the conceptual relationship between brands and customers. In studies by Interbrand, a leading global brand consultancy, the brand equity of global powerhouse brands like Coca-Cola and Disney constitutes upwards of 60 percent of the market capitalization placed on their parent companies by investors. For Coca-Cola and Disney, in particular, the value of the brand image alone is in the tens of billions of dollars.

As a result, Kodak's yellow box, McDonald's golden arches, and Cadillac's distinctive shield became billion-dollar symbols that people could trust to be a promise of a consistent experience: *If you liked me last time, I can guarantee you'll like me this time, too.* The great irony of these symbols is that, in and of themselves, they have little or nothing to do with the products or services they promote; they are simply images. That association would change in the next stage of the digital customers' evolution, the Marketplace of Products, when differentiation became inextricably linked to the essential functions of the products the brand symbols represented. Image wasn't dead; its role simply progressed to support what mattered most in customers' minds: product features.

THE MARKETPLACE OF PRODUCTS

If the marketing battle cry of the Marketplace of Image was "Advertise more!" the marketing mantra of the Marketplace of Products was "Give them more!" The nature of digital technology created purchase considerations that guided people to focus on the products themselves—what they were and the functions they could perform and what other companies supported the functions. In the process, sources of differentiation evolved dramatically, from manipulating and building upon images of a brand's *past* to focusing on what these new products could do in the *present*.

As customer expectations for digital products and services evolved in this next stage, during the 1980s it wasn't unusual to see Bill Gates, Steve Jobs, Craig

McCaw, Michael Dell, Borland's Philippe Kahn, Electronic Arts's Trip Hawkins, Andy Grove, or Lotus's Mitch Kapor engage in product shoot-outs with their competitors at industry conferences and trade shows. Looking back, it's almost comical to remember how audiences gawked over word processing features and vendor shoot-outs at trade shows like Comdex or at technology guru Esther Dyson's PC Forum conferences. So involved were top executives in some of these "feature wars"—as pundits referred to this high-tech battlefield—that Larry Ellison personally wrote the advertising copy that outlined, feature by feature, why his company's database was more effective than that of its nearest rivals.

An entirely new vocabulary was invented, or imposed (depending on your point of view) by the proliferation of digital features. As a tactic to differentiate features, companies tried to translate their technologies and products into things people could grasp and understand, sometimes succeeding, most times failing. Megahertz, graphical user interface, cells, pages per second, dots per inch, transactions per second, RISC, kilobits per second, protocols, 32-bit, 64-bit, roaming, file format, C++, objects, and countless other terms are now part of the everyday conversations associated with purchasing digital products and services.

We conducted research on behalf of Dell in the late 1980s that identified product reviews in magazines as the most important influence on people looking for information related to their product purchases. Because the complexity and the associated arcane vocabulary of digital technologies were hardly intuitive, businesses and consumers alike needed experts to explain all of these digital terms and concepts. An entire publishing industry was created to cater to the increasing numbers of buyers of digital products and services. Publications for consumers and business and technical buyers arrived, including *InfoWorld, PC Week, PC World, PC Magazine, Byte, Datamation, Computer Systems News, Computer World, MIS Week,* and hundreds of other magazines and newsletters. Most were packed with product reviews, including feature charts and grading systems. In turn, these same charts would make their way into the omnipresent ads that filled the magazines and the "spec sheets" available on the shelves next to the computers and peripherals at the local Businessland or hobby house Fry's Electronics.

Marketing the Present

All of this focus on product features existed because of a fateful set of business strategy decisions by IBM in the early 1980s. When IBM introduced the IBM PC in 1981, Apple Computer, the established brand of choice in the fledgling market for personal computers, sponsored ads welcoming Big Blue to the market. However, within two years, IBM would wrestle market share leadership from Apple. And while IBM executed some pretty creative ads for an old-line corporate giant, such as the early Charlie Chaplin ads, which glorified and demystified the personal computer at the same time, nothing had more impact on Apple's market share than IBM's choice to build the PC with help from Microsoft and Intel.

In its decision to use standard components from other companies, IBM created the market conditions for an open product model, which at its core separates everything digital from almost all the products built and marketed for the Marketplace of Image. This open product model is the essential reason behind the two unique purchase considerations of digital products and technologies, as we mentioned earlier: digital products are never finished and never stand alone.

DIGITAL PRODUCTS ARE NEVER FINISHED. In the Marketplace of Image, brands were built on reinforcing a consistent, subjective point of differentiation over periods of time, with brand messages enduring, sometimes for decades. Tinkering with the message was possible, but it often brought unpleasant results. When Campbell's Soup said "Mmm, Mmm . . . Good" was now "Mmm, Mmm . . . Better," sales fell. The New Coke experience, of course, has become an infamous example of branding that veered from the tenets of differentiation established in the Marketplace of Image. Campbell's and Coke alienated customers by tampering with the only thing that truly differentiated them from their competitors—the static, never-changing emotional currency of their brands.

On the other hand, in the twenty years since Microsoft and Intel formed the core of the PC, each has introduced dozens, if not hundreds, of versions of the PC's operating system and microprocessor, respectively. Microsoft has changed the PC's operating system at the architecture level about every five years, and with it, the name, value proposition, and distribution strategy of the product.

As a result, instead of wondering, "Will this product satisfy the expectations I have from the last time I bought it?"—which typified the marketing challenge from the Marketplace of Image—buyers of PCs started asking new questions, based on their new expectations: "Will this product keep up? When is the next upgrade? How can I trust that the upgrade is worth buying?"

In the late 1980s, companies viewed "upgrading"— that is, stimulating sales through the introduction of incremental improvements to an existing product—as a revenue and market share strategy, and Wall Street popularized the idea in earnings analyses. Borland targeted Lotus, WordPerfect, and Microsoft with competitive upgrade promotions; even stodgy HP offered trade-ins on upgrades to Sun servers and IBM mainframes. Nintendo and Sega traded places every year or two by introducing one-upped versions of their respective gaming platforms. Motorola made the latest phone a necessity with the cool-looking analog Micro-Tac and then the even cooler looking, but digital, Star-Tac.

By the end of the 1980s and the early 1990s, upgrading became a defining purchase consideration of the digital product model. It served to cement in people's minds the idea that digital products are perpetually unfinished and always subject to interoperability considerations. The process of upgrading a software application or a new PC was never an isolated event confined to just a Borland database or the next version of Windows's precursor, DOS. Everything—the chip in the PC, the existing files and other applications, the amount of memory available, the size of the hard disk, the software for the printer, the network card or connection to the local area network—was affected by any important upgrade to the computer it-self or the software that ran on it.

DIGITAL PRODUCTS NEVER STAND ALONE. In the Marketplace of Image, products naturally worked well together. Cars ran on gas from any gas station. Different brands of film fit in cameras without any hassle. Any detergent worked in any washing machine. Any kind of paper worked with Xerox machines. Every match could light a cigarette. Plug any phone jack into the wall and there was an instant dial tone. Shaving cream worked with any razor.

But digital products don't work easily together—despite the logical, on-off nature of digital technologies and the role of open standards. The complexity of digital technologies and, increasingly, the competitive politics of the companies that supply them have heightened the difficulties of making products work together. In addition, almost all digital-based applications are an amalgam of components and products from different companies working together to make up the application. The PC provided people with a straightforward mechanism for judging differentiation in the multicompany, interdependent digital product model and established the market conditions for ecosystems as a source of differentiation in our momentum model.

As the 1980s came to a close, the notion of an IBM-compatible PC morphed into the Wintel-compatible PC—the result of a thriving third-party hardware and software industry created to support the DOS/Windows operating system and the Intel 286, 386, and 486 microprocessors. Third-party support established in people's minds a tangible source of differentiation for a particular class of products; Microsoft and Intel built their strategic market positions on this support. The other big market share and investment winners in the Marketplace of Products—such as HP, Oracle, Adobe, Novell, Sega, Compaq, Nintendo, Nokia, EMC, Sun, and others—leveraged these third parties as brand extensions in support of a differentiated position with customers. In the end, the best and most important features of a product were defined not on a pure point capability, but on *total* capability. The likelihood of switching from an existing product category leader to a challenger was most often determined by how valuable the third-party support was to customers, and whether it was too expensive or too much of a hassle to give it up or modify it.

We knew from market history that in the Marketplace of Image the best products rarely owned the most market share—the best *brands* did. The best products didn't win in the Marketplace of Products, either—just for different reasons. As much as Microsoft, for example, tried to convince users that its software features were as easy to use and intuitive as the Macintosh's, third-party support did more to buttress and grow Microsoft's market share versus Apple than anything Microsoft did technically. It was no coincidence that when Microsoft or EMC or Nintendo introduced a new product, a raft of third-party supporters populated the entire purchase process—at the launch, in the store, in ads, and during financial briefings. Digital customers had begun to recognize this kind of support as a source of differentiation in the context of a particular product category. Even in 2002, after *Time* magazine featured a Macintosh computer on its cover, a reader's letter to the editor on the article echoed two decades of Microsoft's advantage over Apple: "The iMac is cute, but after cute, then what? At my local computer store, Mac-compatible software titles are vastly outnumbered by those for the PC."[2]

THE MARKETPLACE OF IDEAS

The proliferation of communications and networking products and services in the second half of the 1990s catalyzed the transition from the Marketplace of Products to the Marketplace of Ideas. E-mail and cell phones tapped into the basic human need to communicate and integrated digital technologies into our daily lives. For the first time, people who weren't trained professional technologists could imagine the possibilities of digital products and services to transform everyday business processes and functions as well as consumer lifestyles.

The spread of the Internet to all walks of life is well documented and we won't repeat it here, but fundamentally the Internet shifted the focus of huge numbers of people beyond incremental features to the possibilities of products. Web surfing, cell phones, and instant messaging in consumers' lives, as well as e-commerce and B2B applications in businesses, became *essential* to people. As a result, everyday people became technology decision makers. In business, for example, information technology spending as a percentage of capital spending among U.S. businesses reached 40 percent by the end of the 1990s. "Once that happened," says Cisco CEO John Chambers, "information technology was no longer an expense item. Instead it became a tool for profits, cash flow, and productivity for every functional area of any business."[3] In turn, business professionals and functional leaders became technology decision makers, willingly and unwillingly, as their budgets contributed to the investment increase. Though the capital-spending boom of the late 1990s has receded significantly, information technology spending is unlikely to exclude business professionals and functional leaders any time soon.

In the home and life, digital products and services have turned consumers into technology decision makers, too. At an industry conference hosted by pundit Stewart Alsop in 1999, research was presented that showed the most important reason parents bought personal computers was to get their children on the Internet, because their "future depended on it."[4] In Thailand on Valentine's Day in 2000, teenagers overwhelmed Bangkok's wireless network with instant messages to loved ones. In Tokyo, instant messaging was also challenging long-held cultural norms of social interaction. As these few examples—along with many others from academia and the popular press over the past five years—illustrate, digital products and services are both ubiquitous and deeply involved in solving problems in business and in people's lives.

As these experiences multiplied, the digital mindset matured to a new threshold: Differentiation evolved from what *products* do—features and functions—to what *people* can do with them to solve business or lifestyle problems.

It was on this point that we decided to synthesize what we what we had learned about the digital mind-set and our effort to understand inevitability as it exists in people's minds. We summarized our findings this way: First, digital products have two intrinsic qualities that separate them from all the analog stuff—they are never finished and they never stand alone. Next, as people's experiences with digital products evolved, these intrinsic qualities became the essential purchase considerations for just about anything digital. As a result, people developed expectations peculiar to those products. The list of these expectations wasn't particularly long: From what we observed in our case studies, four consistently appeared to define the key factors to differentiation in people's minds when surveying the digital choices before them during the purchase process.

1. *Value proposition.* The relevance of any digital product's value proposition to customers evolved from what *products* do to what *people* can do with them to solve business or lifestyle problems. Thus, people judge the superiority of a digital product or service in the context of accomplishing some task or goal of personal or business importance, and they assign technical superiority to the product or service that they perceive to best solve their problem: *My*

definition of what's best is what helps me the most, not what always works best.

2. *Third-party support.* The complexity of the interrelationships among open standards, products, technologies, and companies hastened significantly since the IBM PC. The amalgamation of companies required to create a customer application or service, like e-commerce or instant messaging, resembles alphabet soup. People look at the array of digital products and intuitively recognize that third-party activities validate the value of a particular product category versus other categories in the soup and distinguish the category leader as key beneficiary of the third-party support: *I trust my biggest headache to the most likely solution, and I believe the most likely solution has to take advantage of the best overall capabilities out there for my problem or it wouldn't be the most likely solution.*

3. *The future.* Next year, next month, maybe next week, the offering will change, gain on, or fall behind the technology curve. The customers know it, and so does everyone else. Consequently, when people consider choices, the sustainability of a product's differentiation on a forward-looking basis is as fundamental

an emotional conviction in people's minds as memories were in the Marketplace of Image. Inside people's heads, it's as if every purchase order and receipt subliminally asks: *I know I'm buying an implicit futures contract with this brand. Is there any reason to doubt how long I can count on this company and its products to solve my most important problems?*

4. *Trust.* Trust can no longer be symbolized by a static image; a paper guarantee just isn't enough anymore. The price of a big idea is that it comes with a higher burden of proof before trust can be earned: *"Don't just tell me how much I can trust you to solve my most important problems. Show me some tangible signs that your way is the right way."*

We closed the discovery phase of our research process on these points. We were confident that these expectations captured the digital mind-set. The next step was to design our research model to quantify our hypothesis around the mind-set of inevitability. It was time to get on with the job of building a marketing model to help companies harness the market forces unique to digital products to build and sustain a differentiated position with customers.

CHAPTER 2

The Billion-Dollar Formula

WHILE WE WERE PREPARING for our quantitative research, our boss at Cunningham Communication, Andrea Cunningham, attended a board meeting of First Floor, a young software company in Mountain View, California. To get closer to the burgeoning software industry, Cunningham had recently invested in a highly regarded venture capital fund called Mayfield Capital, a First Floor investor, who had named Andy to First Floor's board.

Sitting next to Andy at the meeting was Bill Davidow, a successful entrepreneur, venture capitalist, and author of several best-selling management books, including *High-Tech Marketing* and *The Virtual Corporation*. Davidow saw First Floor's potential to become a significant player in the software marketplace and, like us, he was trying to understand why and how certain technology companies separate themselves from the pack of competitors vying for a differentiated—and more highly valued—position with customers.

"You know," he said after the meeting was under way, "wouldn't it be terrific if there were some sort of method . . . some sort of *formula* for becoming a market-leading company? I know people who would pay millions for it . . . correction—*billions.*"[1]

This wasn't the first time that someone had mentioned to us the idea of creating a formula to capture and manage the digital mind-set. Operationally, we hoped our research would help us create a prescriptive marketing model—something to put the specific tactics Larry Ellison had mastered into a broader, repeatable set of market actions that would consistently produce results with customers. Our "billion-dollar formula" had to do three things: 1) measure a brand's position vis-à-vis its competitors in the customer's mind; 2) diagnose the strengths and weaknesses of the position; and 3) develop a plan of action that would improve the quality of the brand's differentiation and, thus, its perceived value from the customer's perspective.

In anticipation of building this kind of marketing "dashboard," we started building our research model by looking for an organizing principle based on the four observations we made in chapter 1 about inevitability and the digital mind-set. In one of our brainstorming meetings, a voice in the room—and to this day, we don't remember whose—suggested that what EMC, Sun, Microsoft, Intel, Nintendo, Oracle, Nokia, Cisco, and the other market winners had in common was *momentum*. Momentum instinctively felt like something a company, like any body in the universe, should have. It was frequently used to describe stocks, politicians, and sports teams, especially those on the threshold of success—where success seemed *inevitable*. Momentum also described hot companies, especially in the investment community, where it had a technical definition based on a series of consecutive quarters with increasing earnings.

Momentum also captured the sense of motion surrounding digital products. Products never seemed to move in any absolute direction for more than four or five years. And it wasn't just the pace of technological advancement; the rapid evolution of value points— for example, chips, operating systems, applications software, networking, servers, printers, storage, video game platforms, and many others—brought swarms of companies and venture capital dollars into the market. We knew the digital product model was intrinsically dynamic, and momentum comes straight from the field of mechanics and the study of dynamic conditions. Best of all, momentum already had a formula associated with it—*Mass × Velocity*. By breaking down velocity into its two discrete components, direction and speed, we translated that formula into an equation that more clearly defined the dynamics of the digital mind-set:

$$Momentum = Mass \times Speed \times Direction$$

DEFINING MOMENTUM

The next step in the process was to hypothesize a way to measure momentum with digital customers, based on what we had learned in the discovery phase of our research. We defined the terms in the equation as follows:

- *Mass:* A product's value proposition and its role in the industry value chain
- *Speed:* A company's ability to "get there" faster or keep up the pace of technology change
- *Direction:* A customer's process of coming to trust a brand's ability to know and articulate where it *and* the market are headed in the future

We developed a battery of questions around mass, speed, and direction designed to reveal whether a company had momentum—as our experiences fighting Microsoft, Intel, Sun, Oracle, and all the others had taught us—and *how much*. From an initially exhaustive list, we eventually formulated fifty-seven questions, all relatively simple, requiring only "yes" or "no" answers. The questions included, "Does the company tend to be in partnership with high-quality companies?"; "Is the company shaping the future of the category?"; and "Does the company have leaders who could be called 'visionaries'?"

To test the appropriateness of these questions, we prepared a comprehensive market survey involving nearly two thousand digital customers nationwide, sampling everyone from consumers to CEOs. Then, with the help of a respected market research team, we tabulated the responses and built a prototype momentum model. (That initial database, as of this printing, has grown to more than twenty thousand interviews with business and technical decision makers as well as consumers; and more than sixty different companies and brands including Apple, AT&T, Cisco, HP, IBM, Intel, Kodak, Lucent, MCI, Microsoft, Nokia, Nortel, Sprint, Sun, and others.)

We designed a model to yield a "momentum score" from 0 to 100, indexed relative to the statistically weighted value of the individual attributes. These scores could be used in a number of ways: first, as a quantifiable, numerical measure of a company's momentum based on what customers believed about the quality of the differentiation for a company and its products; second, to compare the momentum of competing companies such as Motorola and Nokia; and third, to compare companies in different markets—a comparison of Intel to Intuit, for example.

At about the time of the initial market survey, Sprint hired us to help position its brand for the emerging Internet economy. Sprint's challenge was to interpret its marketing in the emerging digital context of its markets. We presented our initial momentum model to Richard Smith, a key member of the company's management team, who saw the momentum model—though still in its formative stages—as a compelling way to help Sprint in its efforts. He decided that Sprint would participate in our initial survey and help validate the model. This decision significantly bolstered our data with a real-world application of our model.

THE OUTCOME

The initial market research yielded two important results. First, while the premise for this research was to capture consistency in how people felt about a company's potential inevitability and its momentum, there was also remarkable consistency in respondents' opinions about companies and their attribute ratings. Digital customers shared the same instinctive sense of which companies had momentum and which did not, and a relatively small number of attributes captured this alignment in a powerful—and, we hoped, repeatable—methodology. In research terms, our goal was to have a high degree of confidence in the explanatory power of our model. The consistency of our findings provided that explanatory power, as our research partner confirmed for us, as well as the credibility we needed for the accompanying marketing dashboard we planned to develop.

Second, the overall momentum score, originally designed only to capture the overall alignment in respondents' scores, proved to have a remarkably high correlation—more than 90 percent—with two other, better-established perceptions; namely, future purchase intent and the likelihood of recommending the company's stock to a friend. The data corresponded with Stephen Hawking's two characteristics of good theories, as we mention in the introduction: First, we think our momentum model explained a large field of observations; and second, it appeared to have predictive power about future observations. More specifically, we identified what was universally held in the minds of people specifying and buying digital products and services, and our model correlated closely for them to more traditional and fundamental ideas of buying products.

CISCO'S MOMENTUM

In early 1997, flush from our initial market survey, we decided to fund a new round of research to further refine the momentum model and our ability to analyze the findings. In looking across the technology arena, we uncovered one company in particular that stood out as the right one to study: Cisco Systems. Back then, Cisco was one of a triumvirate of companies, with Bay Networks and 3Com, competing for leadership in the Internet routing and switching wars. Cisco had already claimed the number one position in routing and was number two in switching. Furthermore, it had succeeded in widening the gap between itself and its competitors every quarter. When intelligent routers emerged as the devices that would power the growth of the Internet, Cisco seemed poised for ascension to the next level of leadership.

Cisco CEO John Chambers had made it clear to his management team that his goal for Cisco was to be "one of the most influential companies—ever."[2] For about a year Cisco had been positioned as the third leg, along with Microsoft and Intel, on the stool of marketplace leaders driving the Internet—in effect drafting off *Microsoft's* and *Intel's* market positions. We had even coined a phrase, *Wintelco,* as a way of describing networking (and Cisco's leadership) as one of the key enablers of the Internet. And while magazines like *Fortune* actually positioned Cisco in context to "Wintelco," repeating it verbatim, the company's stated position didn't capture the essence of what gave Cisco the potential to seize market leadership from its traditional competitors as well as emerging ones such as Nortel and Lucent.

Our earlier experiences with HP, Kodak, IBM, and Motorola had convinced us that it was impossible to manipulate a brand's differentiation by coming up with more creative words, tag lines, or stunts than the next brand. That approach worked for product categories like vodka, where brands like Absolut were invented through advertising and the product itself was secondary. The intrinsic qualities of the digital product model demanded a different approach.

FIGURE 2 - 1

Brand Momentum Index, 1997

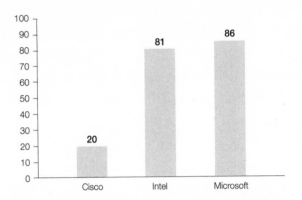

We showed our initial momentum results to Keith Fox, Cisco's head of marketing communications, and Bob Michelet, the company's head of public relations, in November 1997. We had many interesting insights on Cisco's brand position relative to Microsoft and Intel. The most of important of these was that Cisco was not even close to being perceived by its customers as having the same momentum as Microsoft and Intel, the Wintel part of Wintelco (see figure 2-1).

Fox and Michelet are sharp guys, and Cisco is a results-oriented company. So we weren't surprised when Michelet asked, "So what do we do about improving our momentum?" Unfortunately, we didn't yet know the answer. While the momentum model demonstrated that Cisco, on an absolute basis, lacked the perceived leadership profile of Microsoft and Intel, it had no clear channels for addressing the specific aspects of differentiation with which Cisco struggled.

In order to be prescriptive, the model had to evolve. It had to avoid what the brand tracking studies offered—a seemingly endless list of questions about customer perceptions, with little in terms of instructive insight.

Michelet commissioned a second study on the spot. We agreed to focus on turning the model into a prescriptive tool to determine how Cisco could execute a momentum-building strategy.

Finally, we had some momentum of our own.

FROM DATA TO INFORMATION

Less than a month later, the need for a precise prescriptive model for managing Cisco's momentum became even more acute. In December 1997, Chambers summoned us to meet with him. He was frustrated and upset with Cisco's positioning. Cisco's main rival, Bay Networks, had released its annual report using nearly the same words on its cover as the theme of a major presentation Chambers had just given at Comdex in Las Vegas.

"The Internet changes the way we work, live, play, and learn" was a broad vision of the future that Chambers himself had a hand in developing, and it remains Cisco's vision statement to this day. But for a small moment in time, these ideas "belonged" to Bay, rather than to Chambers, and he would have none of it. "I absolutely *refuse* ever to be behind in the marketplace," Chambers insisted.

The momentum study had the ammunition to help him. It demonstrated that a vision that resonates with customers has two parts: the content of the vision and the personality to deliver it. The research was showing that compared to Microsoft's Bill Gates and Intel's Andy Grove, Chambers wasn't on customers' maps. But Chambers couldn't process the research; the results were too scattered. The model had to be more precise and action-oriented to give Cisco the information it needed to get and stay ahead.

THE SIX FORCES OF DIFFERENTIATION

Leaving Chambers's office, we knew we had considerable work to do before the momentum model could provide the type of intelligence Cisco was demanding.

Over the next few months, we looked at what the research revealed and began clustering the original questions into distinct dimensions of differentiation corresponding to the momentum components of mass, speed, and direction. Using statistical techniques, we collapsed the original fifty-seven individual questions into six distinct attributes, which we called the six forces of differentiation. Instead of a repository for a large number of individual data points, each of the six forces represented both an attribute to be managed, leveraged, and manipulated to create momentum, and an indicator of a company's existing strengths and weaknesses as a momentum brand.

The six forces of differentiation also offered a marketing dashboard for companies competing for digital customers. Each force of differentiation represented a dial, like an individual instrument panel on the dashboard of a car or airplane, to be turned up and emphasized or maintained as competitive needs required. Furthermore, as we would later learn, each force of differentiation also serves as a "communication channel" around which companies can organize tactical execution programs and campaigns.

Perhaps most important, these forces of differentiation provided a way of talking to senior management in tangible terms. Marketing and branding were already abstract concepts and difficult to measure, and the Internet seemed to turn everything about marketing upside down. Having a momentum "vocabulary" became one of the most important ways of helping companies understand how the rules of strategic positioning had changed and how they could take advantage of these changes.

At this point in our development, we still only had two-thirds of our momentum-based operational model. To complete the model, we needed to better understand how the individual forces of differentiation supported each other in a momentum product or service strategy, and how to manage various combinations of forces during periods of market opportunity and challenge.

Clearly, the forces of differentiation were not all equally weighted in their influence on purchase intent in the explanatory power of the momentum model (see figure 2-2). In addition, we had seen how Cisco and other market leaders had demonstrated that some combinations of the forces of differentiation worked better than others to sustain momentum with customers over the course of time.

We cover each of the forces of differentiation in chapters 3 through 5, highlighting the prescriptive elements of the model and how companies can manage their momentum using the momentum dashboard. We'll also examine in those chapters how to manage the forces of differentiation in combination to sustain

FIGURE 2 - 2

Forces of Differentiation

	Force	Influence on purchase intent	
	Relevance of Value Proposition	28%	
Mass	Ecosystem Potential	20%	66%
	Category Leadership	18%	
Speed	Market Agility	8%	8%
Direction	Brand Integrity	17%	26%
	Management Vision	7%	

a differentiated position with customers. We'll look at some companies, such as Oracle and Intel, that have managed their momentum so well that they are virtually unstoppable forces with customers, consistently maintaining stunningly high levels of market share and market value relative to even their most ardent competitors.

Here we will give a quick overview of the six forces of differentiation and how they relate to the basic momentum formula. Organized by the momentum variable to which they correspond, the six forces of differentiation are:

- *Brand Mass:* Relevance of value proposition, ecosystem potential, and category leadership
- *Brand Speed:* Market agility
- *Brand Direction:* Brand integrity and management vision

Mass

At the outset of our research, we postulated that mass would be derived from a product's value proposition and its role in the industry value chain. After our research, we defined mass as *the ability to create marketplace value—for customers, partners, suppliers, employees, and investors.* George Foster, a professor at Stanford's School of Business, interpreted our definition of mass this way: "A brand with 'mass' creates marketplace value independent of itself."[3] Scott Cook, the visionary behind Quicken and Intuit, described a brand with mass as having a "system of economics around it."[4]

In our momentum model, in order to build mass, companies must manage three forces of differentiation relative to competitors *and* competing categories of products: relevance of value proposition, ecosystem potential, and category leadership (see figure 2-3).

We examine mass in chapter 3.

FIGURE 2 - 3

Brand Mass

Relevance of Value Proposition	How important is the brand's promise to the personal and professional success of its targets?
Ecosystem Potential	How does the product and its category help other companies make money in a customer solution?
Category Leadership	How dominant is the product's position in its given category?
	How important is the category to solving important customer problems?

Speed

The very fact that all digital products are never finished has ingrained in people's minds the idea that digital products evolve and that, in some perceptible way, the pace of this evolution is accelerating as time goes by.

As a result, momentum brands are always in motion. Executing quickly against industry trends is not enough; they also have to be able to create or manage market transitions to their advantage and respond rapidly to marketplace changes not in their control. A few forward-looking leaders even thrive on disrupting their own incumbent leadership positions. We evolved our initial thinking on what speed means to people and more precisely defined it as those *companies that*

FIGURE 2 - 4

Brand Speed

| Market Agility | Does the company successfully create or manage market transitions to its advantage? |

consistently manage market disruptions, transitions, and inflection points for competitive advantage. In chapter 4 we illustrate the role of *market agility* in managing momentum (see figure 2-4).

Direction

Momentum brands project a sense of manifest destiny even as the market around them changes with greater and greater frequency. This sense of confidence is built on establishing direction; that is, articulating a credible vision of the future and its inherent opportunity for all constituents in a given market space. Following our research, we defined direction as the ability of companies to *anticipate and execute on the inherent market opportunities that come from the impact of technology on markets* (see figure 2-5). Over the past twenty-five years, the most successful visions in technology have been those most closely associated with dominant company personalities: Apple has its evangelist in Steve Jobs; Microsoft relies on the leadership of Bill Gates; Andy Grove's

FIGURE 2 - 5

Brand Direction

Brand Integrity	Does the company practice what it promises to customers?
	Can the company be trusted?
Management Vision	In what way will markets be different because of the company and its products?
	Are the company's leaders credible evangelists for the vision of the market?

vision turned Intel into a force capable of driving the whole PC industry. In turn, brand personalities have come to more closely resemble the attributes of their CEOs than some contrived personality such as a race car driver or a sports figure. This happens because technology is inherently complex and often achieves what would have been thought unimaginable less than a generation ago (such as the computing power of several mainframes inside a video game console). The CEO's role is to make sense of the technology and its potential impact on people's problems for the customers paying for it. Furthermore, the credibility of these personalities—and part of a brand's *integrity*—is ultimately tied to how well the company itself leverages the very technology it is evangelizing to customers. We discuss the implications of direction in our momentum model in chapter 5.

CHAMBERS REDUX

In April 1998—just past our own ninety-day dead-line—we were invited to present Cisco's most recent momentum scores at one of Chambers's executive staff off-sites. During this meeting, Cisco's top players discussed the company's key business initiatives, one of which centered on innovative ways to market the Cisco brand and avoid spending the kind of money Intel—the other hardware giant—had on marketing. Chambers had recently spent time with Andy Grove and had surmised that the brand dollars spent at Intel were daunting compared to what Cisco was ready to spend. Chambers excelled at challenging his company to achieve, in his words, "leverage." This came to mean "$10 worth of results for only $1 spent." Don Listwin, then one of Chambers's top lieutenants, spearheaded this effort earlier in the month. Listwin had seen the results of our momentum work using the six forces of differentiation as our prescriptive framework. It was his idea to present the work to Chambers and his team.

As we waited to give our findings, Listwin summarized the opportunity. Looking at Cisco's momentum results, he told the team, it was clear that the direction of the Cisco brand was job number one. He explained how we had worked together to brainstorm a way to describe Cisco's positioning vis-à-vis Lucent, then Cisco's archrival. This positioning—which would eventually become known as Cisco's "new world" strategy—was the basis for what Listwin wanted to discuss: Cisco's management vision.

Cisco had plenty of room before its momentum came even close to that of Microsoft and Intel, particularly with regard to the relevance of its value proposition to customers. Listwin hypothesized that before the company's value proposition could become relevant in today's economy, it needed to work in combination with the long-term *direction* of the brand in what was becoming an increasingly uncertain and rapidly changing world. The "new world" position, in fact, encouraged a sense of disruption that would only be successful if it was put into a broader context of market opportunity.

When it was our turn, we outlined our results and recommendations. In the middle of the pitch, Chambers pushed back from the table and leaned forward with his elbows on his knees, pressing his palms together and studying our management vision ideas. In a few moments we would get the commitment we had sought for the past two years. In short, our counsel came down to this: If "new world" was the basis for Cisco's strategy over the next several years, Chambers would have to become the CEO of something larger than Cisco, we told him. It required him to become the CEO of the Internet Economy; more to the point, he had to proselytize the idea of an Internet-based economy. If the market opportunity wasn't there, why would the world's largest countries and companies choose something other than the "old world"? In other words, momentum—and the $10-to-$1 return—would have to come from him.

In the next few whirlwind years, Chambers would become known as one of the fastest moving and most influential CEOs of his generation. But at that moment, it felt as if it took a lifetime for him to turn to Listwin and say the words we were waiting for: "Let's make it happen."

MOMENTUM IS LOYALTY

And so we did—for Cisco, and subsequently for dozens of other companies. Applying what we'd gleaned from our database of customer interviews and Sprint's early participation, spurred on by Bill Davidow's timely remark and John Chambers's frustration, we created a valid formula for market leadership, developed a brand momentum index that could quantify a company's perceived momentum, and created an analytic and prescriptive dashboard that companies could use to pinpoint the steps necessary to become a momentum brand.

We would even shed some light on all three of the questions we wanted to be able to answer for our clients: Why do people buy (or not buy) my company's products? Why do they recommend (or not recommend) my company's stock? How can our company do better?

More to the point, what can *you* and your company do *right now* to gain the momentum you need? And once you have it, how can you keep it? manage it? market it? use it to win in the marketplace?

That is what the following chapters are all about.

CHAPTER 3

Building Mass

IN 1998, HEWLETT-PACKARD'S position in the minds of its most desirable corporate customers was increasingly tenuous. On one end of HP's market space stood a rejuvenated IBM and its successful e-business strategy, which had captured the imagination of business executives and the marketplace at large, especially Wall Street and the venture capital community. On HP's other side, Sun had used its Java strategy to mobilize a development community as large as Microsoft's, adding technical value and innovation to differentiate Sun's products effectively and positively against HP's. From the customer's point of view, HP rested squarely between Sun and IBM, lacking an Internet strategy around which the company could accumulate mass and generate momentum.

In 1999, finally recognizing that the classic HP sources of differentiation—its quality track record, engineering acumen, and "good guy" reputation—were no longer enough to win and keep customers, HP launched a new product and marketing strategy called "e-Services." Positioned as "chapter two" of the Internet—after an initial phase dominated by e-commerce—e-Services represented HP's vision of Web-based services that could be brokered dynamically to perform work or complete transactions. E-Services addressed a promising audience for HP: the fast-growing services industries of the global economy. An accompanying software platform called e-Speak supported the e-Services vision, and HP hoped the software platform would attract third parties around which it could build an e-Services ecosystem. HP also hoped all of this market activity would add value to and differentiate its computer, imaging, and services businesses by making them part of creating these e-Services. Finally, HP's dream for e-Services was that it would kick-start a new source of momentum for the company in a way that had been lacking since the mid-1990s, when an exploding imaging business helped HP achieve greater than 20 percent revenue growth for three consecutive years.

One year after the e-Services launch, we researched the quality of HP's momentum with corporate cus-

FIGURE 3 - 1

Awareness of e-Services

Have you heard of the term *e-Services?*

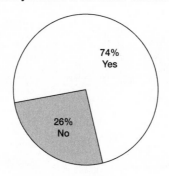

tomers. We conducted the research in two parts: first by examining classic brand-tracking metrics like awareness, consideration, and purchase intent; and second by measuring HP's momentum using the brand momentum index and the six forces of differentiation as our marketing dashboard. The results illustrate how (and how not) to build and manage momentum for a company and its competitive market position.

Our brand tracking research indicated that while HP's customers had strong awareness of the term "e-Services" (see figure 3-1), they ascribed the value associated with e-Services to *IBM* (see figure 3-2). Somehow, IBM had benefited from HP's attempts to build its own leadership profile with the e-Services campaign. But how?

FIGURE 3 - 2

Brand Association with e-Services

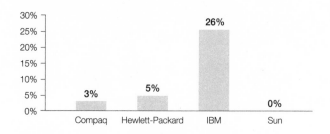

The brand momentum data revealed the unintended consequences of HP's strategy.

At the start of HP's e-Services campaign, IBM had already accrued superior mass around any value proposition that promoted e-business's promise to customers: that new forms of business value derive from the new customer and business connections made possible by the Internet (see figures 3-3 and 3-4). At this phase of the Internet's development, no company, not even a company of HP's stature, could credibly claim a market space positioned within the context of the broad set of e-business value propositions—even as a futures strategy based on an impending, exciting product or technology introduction. HP had fallen behind IBM and then tried to claim ground that IBM had already staked out. Without a relevant source of

FIGURE 3 - 3

FIGURE 3 - 3

Mass

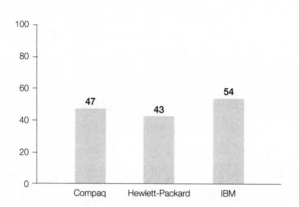

FIGURE 3 - 4

FIGURE 3 - 4

Relevance of Value Proposition

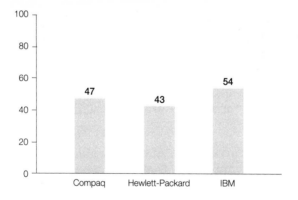

differentiation to distinguish HP's value proposition from IBM's—and to attract third-party support—the campaign failed to build momentum for the company.

The data also revealed the importance of the relationship between the relevance of the value proposition and the management vision, especially in a digital product model that encouraged shorter and shorter product cycles and created frequent opportunities for brands to be dislocated during product transitions. While IBM CEO Lou Gerstner publicly shunned the "vision" word, his prescient e-business strategy, backed by a services-based product strategy, allowed IBM to secure the futures contract associated with the here-and-now value proposition of e-business (see figure 3-5). IBM's advantages in category leadership and ecosystem potential in the strategically important computer server arena had effectively de-positioned HP *before* HP had even launched e-Services (see figures 3-6 and 3-7).

But IBM did not stop there. Once it was in control of both its market position and its momentum, IBM fine-tuned its initial e-business value proposition, narrowing it from one pegged to the whole of e-business to one built on the e-business *infrastructure* required to capture the value derived from e-business. While the ultimate turmoil of the dot-com meltdown hurt almost all brands associated with the Internet, IBM's

FIGURE 3 - 5

Management Vision

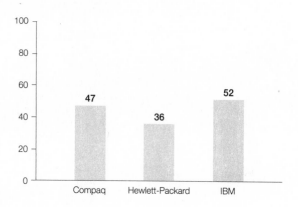

FIGURE 3 - 6

Category Leadership

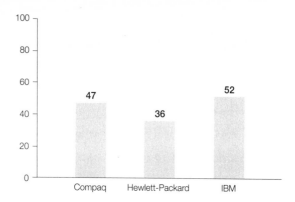

FIGURE 3 - 7

Ecosystem Potential

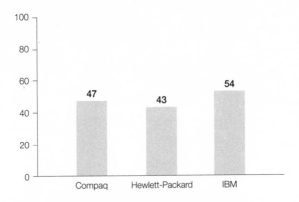

decision a year ahead of the crash to sacrifice and narrow its value proposition around business infrastructure insulated the company from more serious damage. IBM not only demonstrated the courage of smart leadership but also proved the wisdom of giving up something to get something more important. By positioning their technology infrastructure as the most essential source of competitive advantage in a network-centric business era, IBM positioned its servers and integration services as central to its customers' success. In HP's case, the e-Services story proved to be too broad to resonate with customers engaged in building e-business infrastructures. As a result, in the first eighteen months of HP's e-Services campaign, IBM's market valuation rose 25 percent to approximately $200 billion, while HP's declined by about 20 percent to approximately $50 billion.

Not all of HP's market valuation collapse, of course, stemmed from its failed e-Services strategy. Market and investor momentum certainly played a part. But the lesson learned from HP's experience—in short, that a company can't *buy* a momentum leadership position— provides a good framework for discussing how to successfully create and manage a momentum-building campaign.

FUTURE CREDIBILITY

As we noted in chapter 1, people's expectations of companies and products have evolved over the past two decades, influenced by new sources of differentiation and marketplace value. As a result, executing a momentum-building campaign maps to the essential nature of the way customers perceive differentiation: People judge the superiority of a digital product or service by how well it accomplishes something of personal or business importance. The *credibility* of one brand versus another relative to these expectations— and the amount of value people place on a brand—is correlated to the sources of perceived mass: relevance of value proposition, category leadership, and ecosystem potential.

But, like many momentum concepts, credibility has a past, current, and, perhaps most important, future component. *Future* credibility—that is, the perception that a company can advance its superior competitive position into the future—stems from a firm's sense of direction, specifically its management vision and brand integrity. In tactical terms, this means that future credibility requires not only that a company keep its promises but also that it have an external executive champion who can credibly represent those promises—both now and for the future—to customers. Although HP placed a capable, respected executive at the helm of e-Services, the fact that CEO Carly Fiorina arrived at HP after the launch of e-Services and, in her early actions, did not visibly embrace and place her personal imprint on the company's defining Internet initiative gave customers a subtle message about HP's confidence in the strategy. Regardless of whether that decision relied more on timing or lack of vision, HP faced an even greater challenge in building its future credibility without its CEO acting as a shepherd for its vision of e-Services every step of the way.

Future credibility is similar in intent to, although different in definition from, future purchase consideration in that both concepts capture the likelihood of continued loyalty and future product purchases. We will discuss the role of management vision in building future credibility in chapter 5.

STRATEGY OVERVIEW: RELEVANCE OF VALUE PROPOSITION

As we've discussed, the relevance of a brand's value proposition to customers is the starting point for building mass and stimulating the market conditions necessary to create momentum. The problem the brand solves for customers and the particular customer end result that can be expected when the product or service is purchased and used are essential factors to any successful value proposition. Our experience has taught us that positioning a brand to solve a customer's problem is every bit as difficult as cultivating the conceptual image for a brand in the Marketplace of Image or developing the right feature set in the Marketplace of Products.

People expect differentiated brands to solve their toughest problems. Conversely, they expect undifferentiated brands to address smaller problems, resulting in a lower perceived personal relevance and thus lower potential profit margins. In effect, undifferentiated brands are less important and have less potential for building mass. The relative role that mass plays in the purchase decision of a digital product or service is directly proportional to how critical that purchase is to a problem in a customer's life or work.

In the brand momentum model, business customers believe a high momentum supplier is *essential to how they achieve competitive advantage.* Since the era of the IBM mainframe, companies have referred to these buying conditions as *mission-critical.* On a more personal level, customers perceive problem-solving brands as *difficult to live without.* Even in the home, consumers perceive certain digital products as equally mission-critical to their personal objectives. As we noted earlier, many parents believe their child's future success depends on having the right personal computer and getting early Internet experience. This belief places the home computer in a position of incredible personal relevance.

By any marketer's standard, these are high customer expectations to meet, let alone exceed. At an employee meeting, Cisco's John Chambers once talked about the importance of being, in his words, "a great company, perhaps the most influential of all time."[1] But he told the employees that Cisco couldn't become a great company if it didn't solve the biggest problems facing its customers at the time, and into perpetuity for that matter. The key implication, of course, was that solving problems for customers, especially important problems, is not easy, which makes developing supporting product and marketing strategies equally challenging. Brands cannot "buy" a relevant position in customers' minds in the Marketplace of Ideas the way products tailored for the Marketplace of Image can. In that earlier marketplace, Absolut vodka existed as an advertising image before the product was even launched. But in the Marketplace of Ideas, a product must have some combination of ecosystem potential and category leadership to credibly promise a differentiated and relevant value proposition among the myriad of choices available to the buyer.

Sacrifice and Segmentation

We have found that successful momentum brands achieve high levels of relevance for customers by understanding the relationship between two very old-fashioned marketing principles that have been updated for the Marketplace of Ideas. The first is *sacrifice*—the "less-is-more" attribute of any successful brand in any era of marketing. The second is *segmentation*—the means by which a company chooses to target customers. For momentum brands, aligning these two principles is essential to understanding the specific customer problem to be solved, the likelihood of creating value for customers, and the size of the market opportunity. Importantly, this alignment must happen in a way that is consistent with the two intrinsic purchase considerations of all digital products, as we've mentioned earlier—they are never finished and they never stand alone.

The Path to Sacrifice: Usage-Based Segmentation

We would never argue against knowing as much as possible about the characteristics of customers in support of a brand's market position. But in the Marketplace of Ideas, the key to targeting customers is understanding which applications move them to acquire digital products and services and which problems of personal or business importance they hope to solve with those applications. (Applications include PC and enterprise software, e-mail, video games, and the organizing software of PDAs; they can also be inherent to devices themselves, like cell phones or pagers.) We call this *usage-based segmentation*. The point of usage-based segmentation is to group customers into target clusters on the basis of the applications they want and to target the point at which customers experience a solution to their personal or business problems. Later in this chapter we will discuss how different categories of products either enable or directly provide applications, in contrast to other categories that exist in the ecosystems of the application enablers and providers. Customers value these category leaders on the basis of their ecosystem potential—the bigger the better.

In the two years before Bruce Chizen was named president of Adobe Systems, while he was still executive vice president, the most pressing challenge he faced was to integrate the company's disparate product lines and equally divergent customer bases through a compelling product and marketing strategy. Adobe's traditional customer base included publishers of catalogs, magazines, and corporate collateral—all steady consumers of Adobe's products since the birth of desktop publishing in the late 1980s. The Internet brought a whole new group of customers called Web producers, who built Web sites and experimented with interactive media as a means of marketing and communicating to customers. These two professional audiences had little in common demographically and thought of themselves as different types of people, yet both segments depended on Adobe's Photoshop photo-editing software to do their jobs. In addition, tens of millions of people from every corner of the globe used the company's Acrobat or PDF software to create and distribute documents across both the Internet and their own corporate networks in a convenient, consistent format. The Acrobat users mir-rored the diverse population of the Internet universe, most of whom never used Photoshop. The distinct na-ture of Adobe's target audiences, hardly uncommon for successful corporations, challenged the company to settle on a single relevant value proposition around which the company could aggregate these customer segments into a product and marketing strategy that would help it achieve mass.

While Adobe struggled with these challenges in the early years of the commercial Internet, the company frequently battled the perception that it was losing cus-tomers to its key competitors, Microsoft, Macromedia, and Quark. At the same time, its stock price failed to appreciate significantly, at one time dropping so low that industry watchers considered the company a takeover target.

Inside Adobe, the first efforts to redefine the com-pany's market position had focused on Adobe's brand "personality" as a means to manufacture differentia-tion. In the Marketplace of Image, a brand personality represents one of the core means of establishing an emotional relationship with a customer in advertising or product packaging. Adobe's personality exercise ex-plored all the traditional touch points of customer emotion: cars, people, music, poets, and heroes. With so many different customer "faces" to appeal to, however, it was impossible for Adobe to find just a single compelling concept. The brand personality process actually *discouraged* sacrificing to focus on a deep, meaningful promise of customer value, lest some key segment of Adobe users was excluded. Traditional demographics or psychographics, while excellent tools for understanding customers on the basis of their personal or professional characteristics, offered little help in understanding what business problem Adobe's customers had in common. It wasn't enough simply to say Adobe's customers were "creative" or "achievers"—because there were too many different personality types to fit neatly into one or two segments.

When Adobe looked at customers as usage-based segments, rather than as groups of people, Chizen saw the company's opportunity for relevance. In Adobe's customer research, nearly all Photoshop and Acrobat users shared a common frustration: Despite the ubiquity of available communication options—including the Internet, e-mail, cell phones, and pagers—people and companies still found the process of communicating terribly inefficient. Mass communication with customers lacked focus and impact—fewer than one in ten catalogs mailed to people produced a sale. Digital media, while a visually rich, flexible, and promising means of reaching and motivating customers, fell flat in the translation from PC to cell phone screen and, worse, became intrusive in the form of banner ads and interstitials (Internet-based commercials).

When Chizen became Adobe's president, he launched a product and marketing strategy called Network Publishing. Positioned as the successor to desktop and Web publishing, Network Publishing promised to increase the efficiency of communication without regard to device or medium.

"Network Publishing is an era of creating visually rich, meaningful content that is managed and delivered reliably wherever the user wants, whether it's a Web page, printer, cell phone, handheld device or PC,"[2] Chizen said. Network Publishing created completely new classes of services to help customers communicate better, based on customer feedback: "Find-me" print services; scalable graphics technology, which promised to make graphics look equally good on a personal computer or cell phone screen; and Web-based Acrobat services such as e-books were just a few of the new ways Adobe attacked its customers' communications problems with the Network Publishing product and marketing strategy.

By segmenting its customers on the basis of the problems their applications addressed, Adobe uncovered a compelling and differentiated value proposition for its brand. Although it required Adobe to sacrifice other aspects of its brand message, usage-based segmentation allowed Adobe to solve its customers' most important problems and, at the same time, create an integrated positioning framework for all its products, especially the flagship Photoshop and Acrobat franchises.

In developing its value proposition, Adobe also determined that for every $1 customers spent on Photoshop, they spent an additional $4 on products and services from the Photoshop ecosystem, adding significant mass to Adobe's market position. In addition, Adobe signed important new partnerships with HP, Nokia, Amazon.com, and Real Networks that rounded out the realm of capabilities and content made possible by the Network Publishing strategy. The mass that Adobe built around the Network Publishing value proposition created substantial momentum for the company, ultimately helping it to become one of the ten best-performing stocks on Wall Street from 1999 to 2000, according to *Fortune* magazine.

The most successful digital brands have followed this same approach of building mass by addressing customers' most critical problems. Consider these three quick case studies:

- When NTT DoCoMo introduced its I-Mode
  wireless service in Japan, it knew from its success
  in the paging business that such instant communication solved one of the most difficult problems for traditionally shy Japanese teenagers by
  making it possible for the teenagers to introduce
  themselves to one another in a safe and personally acceptable way. The value proposition underlying DoCoMo is so compelling that more than
  one thousand Web sites in Japan offer some form
  of communications service across the DoCoMo
  network, and some studies suggest that I-Mode is
  changing the way an entire segment of the country communicates—all as the result of a specific
  application solving a specific problem. AT&T
  Wireless and DoCoMo are now teaming up in
  the United States, where teenage audiences may
  not be as shy as their counterparts in Japan. Nev-
  ertheless, one survey of instant messaging use by
  U.S. teenagers on cell phones showed that between 15 percent and 20 percent of their messages serve to ask someone out on a date or to
  break up with someone.
- Cisco uncovered an entirely new market opportunity for its business consulting unit by solving a
  business problem for its CFO, Larry Carter. The

advent of the Internet had allowed corporate executives outside the information technology department to envision how Web-based applications
could transform their functional responsibilities,
and Carter had seen the light. Frustrated by finance's gatekeeper reputation, Carter saw the
possibility of closing Cisco's books in less than
twenty-four hours by integrating the necessary
information-sharing across departments and making corporate finance a catalyst for business decision making. What Cisco came to call the "virtual
close" was Carter's goal for the finance department, rather than an IT initiative. As such, it mir-
rored the feedback of Cisco's customers, many of
whom were functional department managers prepared to fund their objectives from their own
budgets. This customer feedback and Carter's goal
for Cisco led the company to begin looking
at marketing, manufacturing, sales, human resources, and other functional departments in
terms of how they figured in customers' common
problem of building Internet-based business
applications. By taking a holistic, cross-department
view of the value it offered customers, Cisco
opened up an entire new market opportunity in
functional department budgets at the same time

its company's sales team targeted customers by the same five major applications—e-commerce, customer care, supply chain, employee self-service, and e-finance—used inside Cisco.

• Watching his wife painstakingly pay the family bills by hand each month, Scott Cook had an idea: Why not write a program that would let people pay bills, track budgets, and print checks from their PCs? Cook's company, Intuit, introduced Quicken, which did just that. Nearly two decades later, more than four million people every month visit Quicken.com to manage their finances. Quicken was more than just a spreadsheet; it was a lifestyle choice that addressed a problem of significant personal relevance in his own life and, as it turned out, in the lives of millions. Quicken offered customers a sense of control over the complexity, inconvenience, confusion, and stress of managing their personal finances. Studies have shown that financial stress between couples is one of the leading causes of divorce. Cook may or may not have known this, but by giving a growing population of young, upwardly mobile, relatively affluent, middle-class PC users the power to simplify and more easily manage their personal finances, Intuit offered relief from an itch that no one else had yet scratched. Intuit achieved so much mass with Quicken that even giant Microsoft couldn't beat them when it tried to enter the same market with a similar product.

KEY SUCCESS FACTORS: RELEVANCE OF VALUE PROPOSITION

- *Segmentation:* Look at your current or desired target customers and determine the top two or three applications that matter most to them. Extrapolate from these applications the specific problems they solve for people and how customers measure their success. Don't get caught up in exercises that try to capture the "personality" of these targets or your brand—they have little to do with projecting a sense of relevance and, therefore, closing a sale.
- *Sacrifice:* Understand precisely what customer problem you're trying to solve and be prepared to give up a lot in order to own a relevant problem in your target customers' minds. No brand can solve more than one or two really important customer problems. Above all, resist the temptation to take every product feature and turn it into a customer problem.

STRATEGY OVERVIEW:
CATEGORY LEADERSHIP AND
ECOSYSTEM POTENTIAL

Digital customers, as we noted in chapter 2, view category leadership and ecosystem potential as the pivotal sources of differentiation when considering the credibility of one brand's value proposition against another's.

In the Marketplace of Image, it was possible to buy a relevant position in customers' minds. Differentiation built entirely or predominantly on a single conceptual image is possible when the capabilities of the product category so resemble each other that form simply transcends function in customers' minds; thus the birth of Nike's "Just Do It"; Camel's "Joe Camel"; and the Shell "Answer Man," among thousands of others.

In the Marketplace of Ideas, however, each of the six momentum-building forces of differentiation—ecosystem potential, relevance of value proposition, category leadership, market agility, management vision, and brand integrity—contributes in its own particular way to how a brand achieves a differentiated position with digital customers. Furthermore, certain forces are profoundly more important from the buyer's perspective when they are leveraged in combination with each other. In the case of ecosystem potential and category leadership, the former is inextricably linked to how much value a customer ascribes to a category of products or services as a source of differentiation. In other words, ecosystem potential can raise the value of a certain category and move it up the food chain in the customer's mind.

This relationship reflects the inherent, interdependent nature of the digital product model, where every product or service category plays a role in solving a customer problem. From the customer's perspective, every category of digital products either enables a solution or simply participates in the solution. In biology, a few dominant species typically control the basis of competition for survival in a particular environment. The same is true with digital products and services when customers divide their investment dollars or budgets into the various categories of products required to build a solution. The greater the ability of a company to genuinely create market value for other companies, the greater the likelihood the category will accumulate ecosystem potential. When this happens, the market conditions will emerge for customers to recognize a brand with increasing mass and to attribute to that brand the marketplace value associated with occupying a highly relevant position with customers. As author and marketing guru Geoffrey Moore says,

"People are attracted to companies with 'market power.'"[3]

To understand the importance of ecosystem potential and its influence on category leadership, consider the case of Novell. From the mid-1980s into the first few years of the 1990s, Novell was the leading supplier of networking software when local area networks (LANs) were the center of the networking universe. At that time, Novell's groundbreaking NetWare software was so popular with customers that industry gurus and Wall Street referred to NetWare as a de facto market standard, not unlike its contemporaries, Microsoft's DOS operating system and the Intel 386 chip. Third-party software called NetWare Loadable Modules and a large universe of channel partners and systems integrators established a thriving ecosystem for NetWare. Companies like Oracle and HP signed strategic partnerships with Novell and committed to developing products in support of NetWare. As a result, the category of LAN software blossomed into a robust driver of market power and market value. At one point in its history, Novell was second only to Microsoft in its ability to influence the market direction of the software industry associated with personal computers and networking.

When the Internet arrived, however, and the vision of a networked world shifted from the LAN to the Web, Novell suddenly found itself in a legacy position with customers. Despite the massive third-party support it had built over the years, the business opportunity of Novell's channel shifted almost overnight to a new generation of infrastructure companies like Cisco, Sun Microsystems, and IBM. Instead of enabling networking, Novell became a mere participant in the larger framework of networking enabled by the underlying technology of the Internet. In short, LAN software's role in customers' minds dramatically devolved to a less important position on the fringes of the extended, Internet-powered network. As Novell's ecosystem dissipated and dispersed, Novell and the category of LAN software could no longer credibly solve an important customer problem. Despite repeated attempts by the company to lay claim to Internet leadership—including hiring Eric Schmidt, one of the most respected visionaries in the technology industry—the relevance of Novell's value proposition beyond the LAN failed to catch on in any meaningful way. Novell never recovered, and the company's market cap and stock price plummeted to levels not seen since its early days as a public company.

The Novell story is especially challenging because the company's flagship product held the dominant leadership position in the category of LAN software and actually possessed compelling mass for at least five years. But Novell failed to foresee the impact of the

Internet and, as a result, failed to manage NetWare's mass and the future direction of the category in any way that proved relevant to its target audience. For insiders in the computer industry, Novell at its peak is remembered for CEO Ray Noorda's obsession with Microsoft and the series of acquisitions he engineered to make Novell more like a desktop software company than a networking software company. The more Noorda's acquisitions focused Novell on Microsoft in PC software, the more customers questioned the company's current and future commitment to its networking heritage at a time when networking was rising to prominence because of the Internet. In short, the company had limited resources to stabilize its past and current credibility, and even fewer to create future credibility.

Some companies refuse to believe that customer expectations have changed and that the credibility of a value proposition depends on ecosystem potential working in conjunction with category leadership. Nowhere is this denial more apparent than in the tales of dot-com marketing fiascoes. By overlooking the fact that their dot-com designations made them digital brands, these companies simply ignored the importance of ecosystem potential in building credibility with customers. From the Pets.com sock puppet to the AskJeeves butler, most dot-com brands ignored evidence that the sources of differentiation for their product or service categories had more to do with their partners and future credibility than with their image attributes and personalities, as in the Marketplace of Image. We once asked the vice president of marketing at Disney's InfoSeek subsidiary what he believed was the most important source of differentiation for Disney's Internet search engine, GO. He answered "logo iconography," referring to the look and feel of the GO Web site. GO launched a major customer initiative, which included a featured position on Disney's new and traditional media like ABC and ESPN, but the site's look and feel alone weren't enough to persuade customers that GO was a superior alternative to competitors like Yahoo! or, later, Google. In less than a year, the company was folded back into Disney.

The failure to recognize the importance of a category's "role" is not simply a casualty of the dot-com era. Many traditional information technology companies have made similar mistakes. Xerox, under a brand image campaign called "Keep the Conversation Going," promised that its copiers and printers could solve the fundamental problems of exchanging and sharing information between people in a networked world. This misguided attempt to reposition the tactile, ink-and-paper brand flopped; it simply wasn't possible for customers to believe that printers and copiers occupied a more important role than the plethora of other product categories claiming to do the same with digital information, particularly Internet browsers and e-mail packages. The lack of third-party support for Xerox's new strategy indicated to customers that Xerox did not really possess the credibility to claim such a position.

"Role" and Relevance

Despite its importance to mass-building, relevance is only part of the equation. It is equally important for momentum companies to manage the role their products and product categories play with customers. After more than two decades of experience with the never-finished, interdependent digital product model, business customers and consumers alike have developed sophisticated expectations for ecosystem potential. In the brand momentum model, customers expect momentum brands to have partnerships with the *highest-quality* companies. Furthermore, momentum brands are expected to help other companies *make money*. Customers look for two signs that a product or service category has the potential to create these market conditions: 1) competition among the supporting third parties of the category; and 2) spontaneous innovation and value-add to the capabilities of the category. Importantly, customers view themselves as the beneficiaries of this competition and value-add—either in the form of lower prices or slower price appreciation, or in more capabilities that reinforce the quality and utility of their technology investment. Careful articulation of your company's unique role in an ecosystem helps to signal your intentions for future importance to prospects and customers.

As we discussed earlier, Adobe's Photoshop customers spend $4 on other Adobe products—such as third-party plug-ins, from special effects software to animation software—for every $1 they spend on Photoshop. The Photoshop plug-ins add significant value to Adobe's franchise product and increase the perceived value of the overall category of photo-editing software among all the software choices available to graphics professionals.

Third-party competition and value-add within the ecosystem create brand extensions. As more and more third parties contend for mind share and add technical value to a category of products or services, the overall market value of the category grows in relation to the size and magnitude of the ecosystem. Sometimes the value associated with certain categories of products accrues exponentially in relation to the overall size or growth rate of the category—as in the case of Intel and Microsoft, and sometimes other companies like Cisco, EMC, and Sun. We believe this happens when companies demonstrate differentiation across all forces of digital differentiation in the brand momentum model. When this happens, companies become unstoppable market forces.

Because of the synergistic nature of ecosystem potential and category leadership, we have found that successful momentum companies almost always manage these two forces of digital differentiation in the same context. When managed independently, the results can be disastrous. That's exactly what happened to SAP from 1999 to 2001.

In 1999, SAP founder and co-CEO Hasso Plattner finally decided that the company needed an investment in marketing to revive the SAP brand, which had stagnated after an almost decade-long run as one of the early pioneers of client-server applications. The market share leader in enterprise resource planning (ERP) software, SAP's market capitalization reached about $100 billion in 1998. Plattner's decision to invest in the SAP brand was prompted by the trend of companies seizing the Internet to redefine the nature of enterprise software. Many of these companies had begun

winning dollars from the IT budgets of SAP's customers. In particular, Oracle, SAP's key competitor,
had finally found its market position after all of CEO
Larry Ellison's fits and starts with the Media Server
and the NC. Oracle was riding the business performance of the Internet-based Oracle 8i database, which
Ellison dubbed "the most important enhancement to
our database in 20 years."[4]

Oracle's flagship database focused Ellison on a single value proposition for the entire company: a promise of radical cost savings brought about by the integration of the Internet into a company's business
systems—which Oracle claimed could only be pow-
ered by an Internet-centric database. Using the premise that the Internet is one large database, Oracle positioned itself to counter SAP's client-server legacy and
the perceived glacial pace of implementing an SAP
R/3 system. The "Oracle can save you a billion dollars" marketing strategy tied to the Oracle 8i product
strategy boosted revenue growth by more than 20 percent in 1999 and 2000, and Oracle earnings hit an all-
time high. Furthermore, Oracle launched a major applications offensive against SAP, which was struggling
to maintain growth and actually experienced a sales
slowdown in the U.S. market at the same time that demand for Oracle was exploding.

In his twenty years at SAP, Plattner had never considered marketing to be the equal of engineering. But this time, faced with the competitive pressures of the flamboyant Ellison and the Oracle brand, as well as upstarts like Tom Siebel and Siebel Systems and a host of smaller players like Ariba and CommerceOne, Plattner shifted gears toward evolving and differentiating the SAP value proposition. With a $100 million marketing budget to spend beginning in early 2000, Plattner repositioned the SAP brand using an ambitious vision integrated with a new product strategy called mySAP.com.

We studied SAP's brand momentum at six months and then eighteen months after the launch of the brand repositioning campaign. The results highlight how ecosystem potential influences category leadership when a company strives to articulate and build credibility for a relevant value proposition with customers, and what the risks are to companies of treating them independently.

Until then, SAP's ERP software was used to manage all the far-flung operations of large corporations, linking the diverse, dispersed components of an enterprise into a single, manageable system. Prior to the introduction of mySAP.com, the company's value proposition was simple: "world-class efficiencies." The company had built its reputation on complex projects to reengineer vital business processes around SAP's R/3 software platform for such Fortune 500 companies as Dow Chemical and Mobil. "The fundamental success of SAP is in removing internal barriers and making corporations more efficient," said SAP's chief marketing officer, Martin Homlish.[5]

SAP hoped mySAP.com would extend this value proposition from the back offices of corporations to every employee's desktop. In effect, Plattner wanted to personalize and put a face on ERP. "We want to be the portal through which businesspeople access everything," Plattner announced. "It's like AOL—for corporations."[6]

MySAP.com ultimately failed to help SAP achieve its goals because of SAP's failure to manage the relationship between the role played by R/3 in the category of ERP software and its associated ecosystem. When we reviewed the year-over-year data of our brand momentum research, we uncovered the flaws in SAP's brand repositioning strategy. To understand these flaws, it is important to recognize that SAP's heritage as the ERP software leader created an ecosystem of business consultants and systems integrators, like Accenture and Deloitte & Touche, who helped SAP's customers map business process reengineering to the capabilities of R/3. The consulting work was highly lucrative, with $10 million in SAP software stimulating upwards of $100 million in consulting and integration services to conceive of and implement reengineering projects. In short, SAP's R/3 helped other companies *make money* and that fact encouraged these third parties to dedicate resources and intellectual capital to SAP.

But SAP's initial television ads in the $100 million campaign to launch mySAP.com failed to hit the right note. They featured golfer Gary Player in a quest for a lost golf club, as well as a businesswoman booking a difficult-to-obtain airplane ticket via mySAP.com. While the idea of extending ERP to the desktop played to the empowerment themes of the Internet, the ecosystem supporting mySAP.com reflected an entirely different set of players than those customers had come to expect with R/3. In addition, golf wasn't a particularly important corporate expense crying out for greater efficiency (or at least few would say so). And while travel and entertainment (T&E) can be important corporate expense items, T&E failed to gain traction as a business problem on par with the significant information technology investments required to manage large complex operating expenses like inventory and a manufacturing supply chain, or tens of thousands of telephone calls to a customer call center.

The initial wave of partners who jumped on the mySAP.com bandwagon complicated the problem by mirroring the end-user nature of mySAP.com. Travel companies and business services like Kinko's offered capabilities that, while important to most companies, were not going to radically lower operating expenses in the same way Oracle promised customers.

The brand momentum data indicated that customers had lost confidence in SAP's ecosystem potential and, accordingly, SAP's relevance as a problem solver dropped in the company's brand momentum scores (see figure 3-8). Interestingly, SAP's category leadership in enterprise software stayed nearly the same, year over year, suggesting that customers failed to appreciate the value SAP hoped mySAP.com would add to the R/3 product franchise.

The postscript to SAP's positioning challenge is Plattner's ultimate recognition of the role of the R/3 ecosystem as a vital differentiator and the key credibility builder for the company's value proposition. Just as we finished our second brand momentum study, SAP abandoned the mySAP.com awareness campaign and created strategic partnerships with CommerceOne and Yahoo! around R/3—improving the quality of the company's perceived relevance and ecosystem and reestablishing SAP's future credibility around the

FIGURE 3 - 8

SAP's Momentum Profile

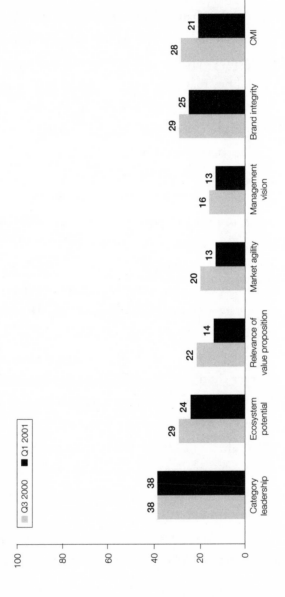

promise of enabling world-class efficiencies. In doing so, the company regained its lost momentum, and its financial fortunes and market performance improved.

Prescriptive Action: Five Roles Are Available in Customers' Minds

In chapter 2, we defined brand mass as the ability to *create marketplace value—for customers, partners, suppliers, employees, and investors.* The most critical contributor to this marketplace value is a company's ecosystem potential.

In our experience, we have observed five general ecosystems that work in conjunction with product categories, reflecting the diversity of digital products and services available to customers, as well as the layered nature of the digital product model. And we fully expect more and different ecosystems to evolve over time; as profit opportunities emerge and business models mature, companies and investors will pursue these opportunities, setting off a Big Bang–like explosion of innovation in the marketplace. Ultimately, an ecosystem supports a "system of economics"—as Intuit's Scott Cook described it—around a specific category of products or services that best sustains the profit-making prospects of this market activity.[7]

Positioning an ecosystem to customers, of course, requires certain conditions to be met in the customers' minds. First, customers have to believe in the potential of a particular category of products or services to play an enabling role in the success of an application that solves a problem of personal or business importance, therefore creating the opportunity for the aggregation of marketplace value around one category relative to others that make up the application. Second, emerging category leaders or enablers must architect product strategies that make it possible for third parties to add value to their products. More simply put, ecosystems grow from business and product strategies that allow and make it worthwhile for third parties to participate in them.

Such product marketing decisions are, in fact, choices for companies and their brands. Despite the open and interconnected nature of digital technologies, some companies prefer to keep their product models as closely held as possible. For most of the 1990s, Motorola strategically viewed the paging industry as a vertically integrated product model in which it controlled as much of the industry value chain as possible. Customers such as Skytel and PageNet, to name a few, were relegated to marketing and customer service organizations, while Motorola supplied the transmission equipment, the software necessary to deliver messages from the equipment, and the devices that Skytel was to sell to customers. In many respects, Motorola attempted to assist each of its customers with technologies to help them differentiate themselves from other Motorola paging customers.

While Motorola was very much aware of the open systems ecosystem of the rapidly encroaching personal computer industry, it consciously attempted to hold back the integration of paging services and the PC world. As the next generation of paging arrived at the end of the decade, Motorola's lack of a robust software ecosystem and internal software competency ultimately contributed to the company's failure to capture the early market opportunities associated with instant messaging and other new Internet-based wireless services across all of the company's wireless products, most notably the company's cell phone lineup. While it is impossible to predict the company's ultimate outcome, its inability to foster an open, healthy ecosystem undoubtedly led to Motorola's precipitous decline in market power and perceived future success.

In the brand momentum model, category leaders must possess three characteristics. First, the brand must have a *large share* of the available category; second, in the markets served, the brand's customers have to be the *highest-profile customers;* and finally, the brand's products have to be perceived as *state-of-the-art.* The credibility of a brand to build an ecosystem around a product or service category depends on the quality of these characteristics. If managed in the context of a relevant value proposition, a category of products and services accumulates ecosystem potential in one of five ways:

The Specialist's Ecosystem: This ecosystem focuses on specific functional improvements to an existing category leader. Almost always incremental in nature, these third-party enhancements help sculpt the overall capabilities of the category leader, adding niche improvements that rarely change the core application. Participants in the specialist's ecosystem must generally adhere to a technical specification, and value-add specialists are positioned as utilities, accessories, extensions, plug-ins, tool kits, and mini-applications. Autodesk's Auto-CAD product platform sits at the center of a successfully crafted specialist's ecosystem. Despite nearly twenty years of market challenges from much larger companies like IBM and Microsoft, the software program for computer-aided design maintains nearly a 70 percent market share with more than four million customers. AutoCAD's dominant market share "has left other CAD com-

panies resigned to developing tool kits and software add-ons for the product," says *Red Herring*
magazine.[8] The more these third parties have contributed to AutoCAD's specialty, the more difficult
it has become for competitors to challenge Auto-
CAD's value proposition with customers. Many of
these unsuccessful challengers have introduced
high-quality alternatives—many of which were
priced at one-tenth of AutoCAD's cost—over
most of AutoCAD's lifetime. But despite major
initiatives from larger, much more diverse competitors, Autodesk continues to enjoy the benefits and
stability that come from a seemingly impenetrable
specialist's ecosystem. Other category leaders with
specialist's ecosystems include Adobe's Photoshop
and Acrobat; Creative.com's SoundBlaster; and
IBM's Lotus Notes, among many others.

The Content Ecosystem: Rather than adding technical value to a category of products and services, the
content ecosystem instead integrates complementary business or consumer content with the business
model structure underlying the category's community of users. A large installed base is required by
the category leader to attract the *highest-quality*
third-party services and content—as defined by one
of the attributes in the ecosystem potential research

framework. Online auction leader eBay has built
the ideal content ecosystem. In 2001, eBay offered
tens of millions of individual products and goods for
sale every day; more than $2 billion of content was
purchased every three months, and its online audience topped thirty million people. Amazon.com has
established itself as the leading online retailer with a
content ecosystem that grew from books to music
to electronics in its efforts to become profitable. The
viral nature of the Internet has allowed content
ecosystems to take on lives of their own, as proven
by the phenomenal, prelitigation popularity of
Napster, and the fact that peer-to-peer networking
sites on the Internet see as many as fifteen million
MP3 music and movie swaps per month, by some
estimates. Other examples of content ecosystem
leaders include Real Networks, Quicken.com,
Microsoft's MSN, and AOL.

The Systems Ecosystem: Often called infrastructure
products, certain categories of digital technologies
provide the underlying capabilities essential to an
application but rarely have a technically visible relationship with the end customer. Ecosystems are
constructed around these categories through the
amalgamation of distribution channels, implementation partners like integrators and consultants, and

technical relationships with other infrastructure providers from adjacent or complementary product categories. The combination of these partnerships forms a system where knowledge, skills, and technical relationships provide a performance advantage and, mostly, a cost-of-ownership advantage over individual point-product competitors—who are often referred to as best-of-breed competitors. When all the resources in a systems ecosystem are working together, the end result is often referred to as architecture, "marketecture," or an end-to-end solution. Cisco possesses the prototypical systems ecosystem. With a multibillion-dollar investment in KPMG and Cap Gemini Ernst & Young to create Cisco-specific integration and implementation specialties; technical relationships with IBM, Oracle, and HP to build special technical linkages into Cisco's networking gear; and the largest distribution channel in the networking industry, Cisco has been able to consistently maintain market share advantages over smaller best-of-breed competitors with less expensive and sometimes higher-performing products. The company estimates that about 850,000 people around the world are engaged in supporting the sales, installation, and maintenance of Cisco's products. Other companies with thriving systems ecosystems include EMC,

IBM, Oracle, SAP, Computer Associates, and Sun, among others.

The Platform Ecosystem: A product category that is capable of supporting a platform ecosystem directly encapsulates the entire end-user experience, unlike a specialist's ecosystem, which operates in the context of a platform ecosystem. The original concept of a platform ecosystem started with Intel and Microsoft, as we discussed in chapter 1. A platform ecosystem manages third-party value-add through the tight control of technical specifications and development tools made available by the category leader. Absolute compatibility on a technical level is an essential requirement of the platform ecosystem, as hundreds if not thousands of disparate components have to work together seamlessly in order to ensure a consistent end-user experience. While Intel and Microsoft are the most often-cited examples of the platform ecosystem, AOL's instant messaging and the Palm operating system are also excellent examples of product strategies that support a platform ecosystem. Both AOL and Palm have constructed broad third-party support for their product strategies, which has enabled both companies to maintain at least twice Microsoft's market share in their respective categories, putting them among the very small group of companies that have successfully built and maintained market share advantages over Microsoft and sustained those advantages over multiple years. Other platform ecosystem examples include video game platforms like the Sony PlayStation and Nintendo and communications services platforms like NTT DoCoMo's I-Mode.

The Open Source Ecosystem: Best exemplified by Linus Torvalds and the development of the Linux operating system, the open source movement encourages free and open distribution of third-party value-add to a product as long as certain technical rules are met. The first wide-scale effort at an open source ecosystem was stimulated by the release of the source code for the Netscape browser. An open source ecosystem encourages a rapid evolutionary process for software, with the idea that thousands of independent programmers can produce better software than a small group of programmers in the pay of a single company. Although an open source ecosystem resembles a platform ecosystem, it develops differently. While the open source ecosystem has technical rules for the way things develop, the lack of ownership of the core technology creates a more spontaneous, interpretive environment for innovation. The programmers themselves make up the core of the open source ecosystem. As more and more development activity takes place and customer implementations in production environments go live, traditional technology companies may lend their support. Linux is the most famous of the open source ecosystems. Several companies, including Red Hat and VA Linux, went public based on Linux-centric business models. IBM, Oracle, HP, SAP, and many other vendors have given their support to Linux. Beyond Linux, other successful open source ecosystems include Apache, which runs more than half of the world's Web servers; Perl, which is the engine behind much of the live content on the World Wide Web; and BIND, the software that provides the Domain Name Service (DNS) for the entire Internet.

KEY SUCCESS FACTORS:
ECOSYSTEM POTENTIAL AND
CATEGORY LEADERSHIP

- *Know your role and prove it:* Determine what role your company and brand play in solving a customer's problem; understand whether your brand enables the solution or simply participates in the solution. Use a concept like Bain & Company's industry "profit pools"—which break down total profits from an industry into segments such as manufacturing and services in order to identify the value-add activities in an industry—as a lens to dissect the profit hierarchy of your key application segments and to identify how to position your category relative to others in the application. Resist every temptation to try to occupy more than one role in solving the customer problem addressed by the application; Microsoft is one of a just a small handful of companies with multiple ecosystems. Engage in numbers-based marketing by peppering customers and third parties, as well as investors, with facts and figures about the size of the brand's ecosystem and the economic potential of the market space. Determine a way to express the size of your brand's ecosystem in the context of the category: How many developers are there? How many dollars do customers spend to purchase all the components required to build or deploy an application? What are the recurring revenue opportunities? How much time do customers spend using a particular product or service? How much money do they spend with the brand or ecosystem? Sun Microsystems executed one of the most effective numbers-based marketing campaigns in the early phase of its Java launch. Called the "Java Momentum" campaign, Sun established benchmarks for capturing the number of desktops or user devices using Java; the status of Java's strategic partnerships with companies like Oracle and IBM; and the size of the development community supporting Java. Primarily a public relations and word-of-mouth campaign, "Java Momentum" had only one goal in mind—to create the perception of a bigger development community than Microsoft's. Benefiting greatly from the network effects inherent in Java, Sun leveraged its Java momentum to create a platform ecosystem around the company's server products that effectively established superior credibility for Sun's value proposition of networked computing over that of rivals like Hewlett-Packard, and established a line of defense to slow Microsoft's encroachment on Unix-based operating systems. Google, Macromedia's Flash, and Adobe Acrobat are other examples of brands that effectively communicate via numbers-based marketing platforms.

- *Encourage brand extensions:* Nothing is more important to the success of a system of economics around a category of products than the quality of

the third-party support and value-add. It's easier
to produce a partner program than it is to justify
the economic opportunity to third parties. In
other words, it's one thing to invite partners to
seminars and industry events; it's quite another to
architect a technical means for people to add
value to what you're doing into your product
strategy. Be clear about the business model
framework and the size of the economic opportunity available to third parties. Make it easy for
committed third parties to show their support
for your product category, either in the form
of brand imagery like logos or in helping to
promote their value-add innovations. Look for
role-model third-party programs like the Adobe
Solutions Network, the Autodesk Developer
Network, the Intel Developers Forum, and the
Sun Developer Connection.

- *Own the "leading indicator" customers:* Every digital
  market takes some measure of direction from
  the group of companies and users who are early
  adopters of its products and services. With a
  higher tolerance of risk balanced by break-
  through expectations, these companies do the
  heavy lifting of experimentation. What works on
  Wall Street, for example, eventually finds its way
  into more conservative but related industries

such as insurance and banking. Author Geoffrey
Moore calls these customers the pins in the
"bowling alley" of market adoption. As the
bowling pins fall, other less adventurous market
segments rush in to adopt a certain digital product or service. In addition to building credibility
for the here-and-now promise of value, momentum brands also cultivate leading indicator customers as key indicators of future credibility.
Historically, financial services, electronics, entertainment, retail, and Internet companies have
been the key leading indicator markets of what
applications matter most to digital products and
services. Build a matrix of the key customer applications in which your product or service category has a credible industry role on one axis (for
example, ERP, CRM, business intelligence); on
the other axis, cross-tab the top five industry segments (for example, financial services, entertainment) with real customer names. Establish
benchmarks of success with these customers—
best practices, case studies, and endorsements—
and establish a means to communicate these
benchmarks to the broader bowling alley of target customers. Public relations, industry events
and trade shows, and market analyst reports are

proven tools for creating word of mouth and
peer-to-peer conversations about successes with
leading indicator customers.

- *Define a product metric to gauge state-of-the-art:*
  One of the key holdovers of the feature wars is
  the desire to understand how to judge superior
  product performance. In one of the most brilliant
  strokes of marketing in the past decade, Intel decided to shift how it measures the processing performance of its chips to megahertz. Previously,
  measures like MIPs (millions of instructions per
  second) or the Norton Utilities Speed Index provided users with processor speed comparisons,
  but the complexity of these measures made them
  meaningful only to power users. Megahertz provided a predictable, linear scale on which customers could judge chip performance. More
  importantly, megahertz could be equated, in
  laypersons' minds, to horsepower in cars, offering
  a measurement that was easy for "regular" people
  (that is, the increasing population of PC buyers)
  to understand. It provided a contextual basis
  for gauging performance—answering customers'
  questions of whether or not they were buying
  state-of-the-art—and laid down a way to track
  future performance thresholds. Finally, it provided

a perceived performance advantage for Intel chips against competitors such as the PowerPC. Like everything successful in positioning a product, sacrifice is key. Understand which single performance metric matters most to achieving a meaningful relationship between a set of customer applications and the role your category plays in the overall solutions. Make sure the metric is extensible over a period of years. Establish an individual management leader as a technology guru and create a personal positioning platform around the individual and the metric, as Sun did with Bill Joy, Microsoft did with Nathan Myrvold, and Netscape did with Mark Andreesen. Engage third parties in validating the metric and benchmark competitors in appropriate customer environments.

- *Know your CEO:* At the beginning of this chapter we noted the importance of managing the relationship between brand mass and management vision and the competitive differentiation created by managing them seamlessly. One of the key aspects of achieving this seamlessness is aligning the profile of a CEO with the type of problem a brand is striving to solve. Since a brand's personality is a more accurate reflection of the CEO's true personality than a contrived set of images, companies enjoy marketing leverage when their value proposition and the CEO's personality are seen as aligned. The precision of SAP's "world-class efficiencies" was the mirror image of SAP's Plattner before the mySAP.com experiment. As *BusinessWeek* noted about Plattner, "When the German software giant SAP runs into a glitch, Hasso Plattner figures it out and fixes it with his own bare hands."[9] The blunt, in your face, "we can save you a billion dollars" promise of Oracle aligns with the pugnacious personality of Ellison. The "aw-shucks," everyday personality of AOL's Steve Case fits perfectly with AOL's "you've got mail" promise of easy and comfortable connections with a community of people. Remember that CEOs are in the limelight every day in today's media-hungry culture. Despite this fact, the goal is not simply to create high-profile CEOs. Momentum companies keep the CEO's personality and the company's value proposition aligned and consistent.

CHAPTER 4

Gaining Speed

"FAST FOLLOWER." That's how Jim Firestone, the general manager for IBM's Aptiva personal computer group in 1998, described the company's positioning strategy for the consumer marketplace.[1] The idea behind the fast-follower positioning was to out-execute its key competitors Compaq, Dell, and Gateway after one or some combination of them announced their product intentions. On pricing strategies, for example, IBM ceded leadership to Compaq and relied on its ability to catch up to a price point within a week or two. IBM tried to quickly match market-defining moments, such as Compaq's drive to be the first major PC vendor to break the under-$1,000 price point.

No matter how fast or how well IBM responded, however, the business model of the fast-follower strategy was fundamentally flawed. The pace of the PC business model accelerated dramatically in the second half of the 1990s. Strategies that might have worked in the early part of the decade were no longer possible. The PC market had reached a point where it was moving so fast that pricing strategies followed the 80/20 rule— 80 percent of the profits at a particular PC price point were captured within the first two weeks or so of the new price threshold. After that time, vendor after vendor in fast-follower market positions—essentially brands whose business models saddled them with slow go-to-market strategies or whose volumes were too low to get early parts from Intel—rushed in to fight over the remaining portion of the profit pool tied to the price point. Within a month, give or take a week, the remaining profit opportunity was virtually nil. Over the coming weeks and months, vendors would create promotional considerations, bundles, and different combinations of products in attempts to create value around the price point. Through all this activity, Intel lurked in the background with new, impending price thresholds and product performance cycles under wraps. Certain PC makers with a proprietary business model edge, such as Dell, were able to take advantage of Intel's cycles more quickly and consistently. Because Dell sold PCs directly to customers, it minimized the lag time between when a new product became available and when customers were able to buy it. Others, like IBM, had to build the product and use weeks of precious time getting it into its traditional channel of computer dealers and mass-market storefronts like Sears or Circuit City. The increasing speed of the marketplace had begun to overwhelm Big Blue. In short, the *market* moved at a different pace than IBM. The other leaders established the tempo of the category around certain price and performance thresholds, making it easy for consumers to slot IBM into the laggard position among the choices available to them. Within eighteen months of Firestone's comments, IBM abandoned the Aptiva brand in the consumer PC space. Eventually, IBM would abandon its consumer PC efforts altogether.

FROM PRICE TO PERFORMANCE TO PACE

The use of pricing as a strategy for differentiation is as old as commerce itself. Pricing is a marketing science, especially for commodity products like consumer packaged goods (CPG). For most CPG categories, brand and economies of scale usually supersede the product's actual capabilities as the key price consideration. Furthermore, because the raw materials in such commodities as detergent, cigarettes, gasoline, and soft drinks rarely change, the attributes of these products rarely change either—sometimes for decades.

Unlike commodity consumer brands, digital products and services have many potential points of differentiation, especially during product life cycle upgrades. But in digital markets, price eventually evolved to mean *price-performance*. In the digital product model, price matters only in the context of the performance characteristics of a particular category of products or services. By the same token, performance is always evaluated in terms of price. This happens because every digital product is likely to go through a significant transition—if not a complete metamorphosis—in its capabilities roughly every year and a half. This phenomenon is the result of "Moore's Law," Intel founder Gordon Moore's prescient prediction that microprocessor performance would double every eighteen months. In some categories, such as network switching, the price-performance transition occurs even faster. In network switching, the price-per-port—the means by which price-performance is expressed for this product category—declines by about 50 percent *every year*. While the performance curve for most digital technologies looks like an "S" curve—up and quickly to the right—the ability to price at a corresponding rate is simply not possible in the digital product model. The reliance on open standards in the digital product model promotes rapid imitation and competition, resulting in a price curve that is heavily discounted, if not negatively discounted, relative to the progression up the performance curve.

As performance goes up and price goes down, the two meet at moments in time to establish a market transition point in customers' minds. These market transition points, repeated over and over throughout the life cycles of products and services, are signals to customers to add new considerations to a purchase decision and to inspect a company's position relative to these considerations.

With increasingly shorter life cycles in the digital product model, it is a given, as we've discussed, that people expect digital products to change, to get smaller, faster, and cheaper. And since all digital products and services eventually become commoditized, the ability of a company to manage transition points ahead of commoditization defines how customers associate speed with one company and not others.

Semiconductor makers set the early standard for the way brands manage the transition from unique products to commodities, and then introduce new unique products. Motorola outpaced other cell phone makers, for example, when it abandoned its "bag phones" to make a deliberate transition to the first generation of flip phones. Later, of course, Motorola lost cell phone market share leadership to Nokia when the Scandinavian communications company seized the technology transition to digital cell phones.

In customers' minds, companies must manage ahead of both the industry and commoditization trends in order to sustain the creation of business or personal value associated with providing a superior solution to people's problems. That is why, when a market transition point occurs, people ask, *I know I'm buying an implicit futures contract with this brand. Is there any reason to doubt how long I can count on this brand to keep up with what's required to solve my most important problems?*

In chapter 1, we defined brand speed as a quality of those companies that *consistently manage market disruptions, transitions, and inflection points for competitive advantage*. In the brand momentum model, brand speed is measured in terms of market agility, or the likelihood that a company can sustain accumulated mass into the future. Digital customers need to be constantly convinced that a company is *leading* the pace of any market transition, rather than falling behind or just keeping up with the status quo.

In times of rapid transition, momentum can be a zero-sum game—for someone to gain, someone has to lose. We observed this phenomenon early in our research. The Netscape initial public offering in August 1995 was a watershed moment, not just for Netscape, but also for Microsoft's perceived momentum, especially among those in the investment community. Not long after the IPO, influential Goldman, Sachs analyst Rick Sherlund hosted one of the most highly attended analyst conference calls in history. In the course of the two-hour-plus conversation, Sherlund essentially said that Netscape's browser and its HTML-based Internet browser environment offered a parallel universe to Microsoft's well-entrenched corporate computing environment. He then went on to suggest that the alternative, Internet-based environment that Netscape would help enable might just evolve and grow to represent as large an opportunity for software developers and infrastructure builders as Microsoft's ecosystem. Within two weeks of Sherlund's call, nearly a billion dollars disappeared from Microsoft's market value, while roughly the same amount appeared in Netscape's market cap.

Sherlund was careful to define the opportunity as incremental to Microsoft's existing franchise. But the investment community knew that upon recognizing the potential of this emerging ecosystem opportunity, the relatively finite number of software development organizations would shift some meaningful percentage of their development resources toward this new arena. They also knew that while the economic opportunity of Microsoft's potential business was not affected, its capacity to be seen as leading industry trends was compromised.

Netscape's success represented an erosion of Microsoft's market agility and, for a moment in time, froze the company's market position in many customers' minds. However briefly, Microsoft's inevitability wobbled. At the same time, the vision of Netscape's success flared with an intensity that reflected the potential of the market as a whole; its potential to build mass was significant. We'll discuss in the next chapter how Microsoft misjudged the way customers expect companies to build market agility, including how people have evolved their expectations for a trusted brand in the form of brand integrity. Microsoft's miscalculated bet that it could buy market agility through a television advertising campaign featuring Bill Gates and Steve Ballmer declaring "the best is yet to come" in software innovation, combined with its poor showing at the Department of Justice antitrust hearings, backfired and stalled Microsoft's market position until Internet Explorer emerged as a credible rival to Netscape Navigator.

STRATEGY OVERVIEW:
MARKET AGILITY

We noted in chapter 2 that the likelihood a company could keep up with or even lead the pace of a market is as fundamental an emotional conviction in people's minds as memories were in the Marketplace of Image. In the context of sustaining momentum and maintaining a differentiated position with a customer, market agility contributes to easing the natural human doubts that exist when the tempo and the impact of change are unpredictable. We have found that momentum brands manage market agility to satisfy a portion of the futures contract that comes with every digital product or service. We also believe that brand integrity complements market agility in addressing whatever new considerations customers add to their futures contracts. In addition, market agility has a bidirectional quality that causes it to build credibility for the mass accumulated around a brand. In short, to customers, market agility is a leading indicator of continued satisfaction over the course of a relationship with a brand, and it plays a significant role in the likelihood of continued customer loyalty.

Just as customers have developed a sophisticated sense about ecosystem potential, they have also developed high expectations for market agility. In our research we found that customers and partners assign market agility to those firms perceived to *respond quickly* to new market opportunities, have *cutting-edge business philosophies,* and *take risks* in order to succeed. Interestingly, *Business Week* observed similar sentiments about the struggles of the telecommunications industry, specifically within the context of criticizing AT&T:

> *The biggest mistake AT&T made was to assume consumers would be confused by technology and that they would pay a premium for the services of a trusted company to guide them into the digital era. As it turns out, most people weren't as confused by technology as AT&T executives thought. The lesson is that brands, even great ones like AT&T, must be constantly reinvigorated by new products and services.*[2]

By underestimating the sophistication—and the expectations—of its customers, AT&T held back from the kind of risk-taking and innovation that would have allowed it to maintain its leadership position during trying times for the industry.

In our experience, momentum brands build and sustain market agility by managing the lens through which their customers judge the pace of change in a particular category of digital products and services. As we have mentioned, one of our goals in developing the brand momentum methodology was to create a marketing dashboard with knobs and dials that companies could adjust at certain moments of market opportunity or vulnerability. In the course of developing this analysis we have found that market agility acts as a bridge between the sources of relevance and credibility—that is, brand mass—and the sources of future credibility—brand direction. In essence, market agility acts in concert with the other five digital forces to achieve and manage momentum. Market agility allows companies to create different concentrations of momentum, depending on where competitive opportunities exist and where weaknesses need shoring up. By turning up the dial on brand integrity, management vision, ecosystem potential, or category leadership, market agility can be used by a company to sustain its key sources of differentiation in the context of a customer promise of value.

Market Agility and Brand Integrity

In late 1998, John Chambers had an epiphany that would, in the course of the following two years, dramatically improve Cisco's momentum relative to the company's main rivals, Lucent and Nortel. At the time, Cisco had been urging its customers to build

Internet-based applications in order to improve productivity, and the company had been trying to identify—ahead of customers—the applications that would provide the greatest leverage on that front. Chambers had identified e-learning as a key potential application, but he was having trouble convincing customers that e-learning would be one of the killer applications of the Internet.

"There are two equalizers in life—the Internet and education," he would say with as much conviction and passion as his sales instincts would allow.[3] But while Internet adoption was catching on like wildfire, customers were relatively slow to adopt e-learning, and it was driving Chambers crazy. If he couldn't personally persuade his best customers to bet on e-learning, why would others buy the network gear required to handle applications with as much network content as e-learning? Chambers soon realized that, if he and Cisco represented the same brand promise, then Cisco itself had to adopt e-learning as proof of its value. "If we aren't doing it ourselves," he reasoned, "how can I ask my customers to do it?"[4]

When Cisco's IT staff briefed Chambers on the internal network upgrade required to implement e-learning, he quickly realized that the rollout of the initiative would come in waves, with the scope, potential, and pace increasing with each wave. From these internal briefings, Chambers set in motion a process that would ultimately create Cisco's Internet Business Solutions Group (IBSG), a consulting service to help customers plan the future of their business applications, including next-generation applications such as supply chain management, e-commerce, employee self-services, and e-learning.

In its first three years of deployment, e-learning would become one of Cisco's most successful internal productivity applications. For example, Cisco created an ecosystem of learning partners to help its sales force and channel partners keep up with the company's complex and rapidly evolving set of products and technologies. E-learning allowed Cisco to reduce its hard-dollar outlays for training by 40 percent to 60 percent and to slash the amount of time workers spent in classes (and thus away from their desks) by 80 percent. Cisco also went on to sponsor more than eight thousand Network Academies around the world to create one of the industry's largest e-learning networks. In its history, about 150,000 students have graduated from Cisco's Network Academies.

In responding to Chambers's epiphany, Cisco built credibility for its brand position in two ways. First, the company established a credible and tangible source of differentiation in the IBSG service delivery strategy, combined with an internal best practice to share with customers. Second, with a proven road map, Cisco paved the way for how customers should expect to see the pace of application adoption unfold, including network dependencies. Because Cisco had built and deployed its own e-learning applications, the company was able to credibly help customers plan for the pace of adoption, understand what to expect at important transition points, and anticipate the cultural impediments inside organizations that would need to be addressed to make e-learning work. Later, Chambers articulated a vision for the future of all network-based applications, called the "waves of applications," based predominantly on the company's early experiences with networked applications like e-learning (see figure 4-1).

Our brand momentum research in the networking segment indicated that in the year after Chambers committed to an internal adoption of e-learning to help boost Cisco's productivity, the company improved its market agility and brand integrity advantage over chief rivals Lucent and Nortel (see figures 4-2 and 4-3). In contrast, at a time when Cisco focused on the future trajectory of applications, Lucent focused its communication around a campaign, targeted at Cisco, that asked customers whether they wanted their data networks to be as reliable as their existing phone net-

FIGURE 4 - 1

Waves of Applications

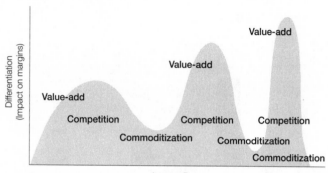

works. Cisco outpaced Lucent, not just because it hit on a powerful means of building credibility with customers, but also because Lucent was still speaking the language of the Marketplace of Products when its industry had already entered the Marketplace of Ideas.

Market Agility and Category Leadership

Perhaps no company has been more effective at managing the pace of its key markets than Intel. The company has done two things remarkably well. First, Intel has benefited from its association with Moore's Law both in perception and in reality; and second, the company has used megahertz and, later, gigahertz, as a price-performance benchmark.

FIGURE 4 - 2

Market Agility

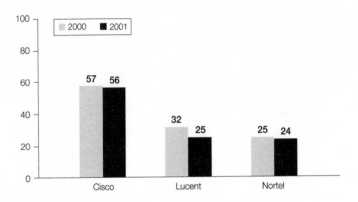

FIGURE 4 - 3

Brand Integrity

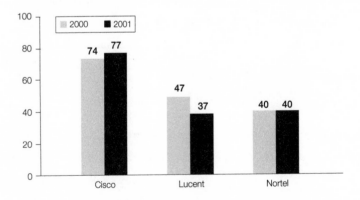

In perception, the law of processor performance provides a simple conceptual framework for customers to anticipate changes in chip speeds and overall performance. Moore's identification with this simple benchmarking tool gives the company an implicit credibility boost and a capacity to set expectations for the category.

In reality, Moore's Law has allowed Intel to manage its product road maps with a long history of consistency. The company openly publishes product road maps as much as a year out and discloses three- to five-year plans with strategic partners (see figure 4-4). Intel is so effective at managing product transitions that the company has a third-party following dedicated to translating its processor introductions into end-customer price points in every market segment it serves. For example, One2Surf.com, a Web site analyzing Intel's road maps, offers the following level of detail and commentary on Intel's road maps:

> *Intel Platform Road Map Update: Pundits have speculated for many months that Intel's insistence on introducing P4 on a high-cost Rambus platform could have a drag effect on its successful early adoption in the market. Intel will be trying hard to enable $2,000 system prices for Pentium 4 PCs. P4 systems are likely to ship with large configurations of the fastest and most expensive PC800 RDRAM.*[5]

FIGURE 4 - 4

IA Enterprise Processor Road Map

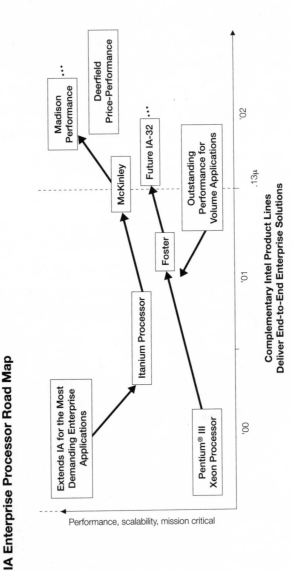

As we discussed in chapter 3, Intel's second key strategy—its introduction of megahertz as a performance benchmark—allowed it to seize control of the ways in which customers measured and evaluated processor performance. Current research shows that people generally base their buying decisions for personal computers on processor clock speed, listed in megahertz. Chip prices also follow megahertz.

Ironically, most experts and industry analysts admit openly that processor clock speed is not a very accurate way to benchmark either processor performance or—more important—computer performance. Yet, as the industry has become more and more comfortable with the notion of clock speed as a proxy for performance, Intel has actually redesigned their architecture or technology blueprint to optimize for megahertz.

The strength of megahertz as a tool for product specification is so strongly ingrained in customers' minds that competitors like AMD and Apple have invested significant resources in trying to discredit megahertz by explaining its flaws. In a defensive move, AMD even abandoned the use of megahertz in its product nomenclature in an attempt to differentiate itself from Intel. By publishing a product road map, in combination with the simple but meaningful product

FIGURE 4 - 5

Intel's Brand Momentum

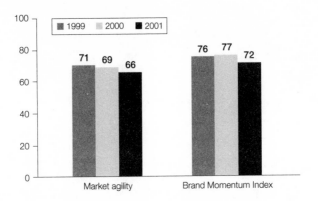

performance specification, Intel sustained its momentum as consistently as any company in our brand momentum database (see figure 4-5).

On the other hand, the lack of a next-generation product road map for the type of routers used for the core of the Internet was one of the primary reasons Cisco slipped against networking start-up Juniper Networks for almost two years. Customer doubts about Cisco's futures contract allowed Juniper Networks to capture nearly 30 percent of Cisco's market share in the category of network equipment known as high-end routers. In the span of less than two years from 1999 to 2001, Juniper beat Cisco to market with a family of routers that operated at a speed called OC-192, or 10 gigabits per second when measured in

FIGURE 4 - 6

Cisco's Momentum Profile

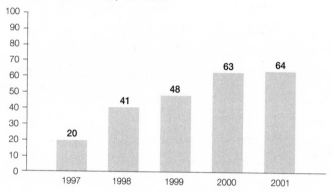

Brand momentum index, 1997–2001

networking terms—a generation ahead of Cisco's OC-48 routers, which operated at just 2.5 gigabytes per second. By setting the pace of price-performance, Juniper created enough customer doubts about Cisco's market agility that Cisco's brand momentum plateaued in the United States for two years (see figure 4-6). Cisco later regained a portion of its lost share, in part by publishing an integrated product road map of next-generation Internet routers that effectively seized control of the industry's performance measurements back from Juniper. "Customers expect a single product architecture with a clear product road map," John Chambers observed in explaining the company's success against Juniper.[6]

Motorola succeeded in dominating next-generation paging in the late 1990s by promoting a road map for its FLEX next-generation protocol for wireless messaging. At the time of its introduction, FLEX was one of a number of protocols being touted as the answer to the industry's need to replace the POCSAC paging protocol with a more powerful, flexible approach. Motorola's success in securing FLEX's role as the dominant protocol hinged on its ability to show the industry a product road map that explained FLEX's role in enabling important new capabilities such as voice paging and two-way paging. By laying out a road map of FLEX-enabled, next-generation applications and offering a protocol that third parties could easily extend to new applications, Motorola succeeded in communicating to the industry that FLEX would allow it to move forward and exploit next-generation capabilities much more quickly than competing protocols. In short, Motorola convinced the industry that FLEX provided a more robust platform for revenue generation, application development, and service to its customer base.

Market Agility and Ecosystem Potential

Real Networks is one of the few companies to face down Microsoft and keep winning customers. Confronted with increasing competition and focus from Microsoft, Real Networks has chosen to defend its leadership position in the media-streaming business by applying the very source of differentiation Microsoft has used so well historically: ecosystem potential. And by pacing the market against this source of differentiation, Real Networks has been able to avoid the fate of other category innovators that have crossed Microsoft's path.

Real Networks took a two-pronged approach to its positioning strategy against Microsoft. First, the company established its file format as the de facto market standard for the distribution of audio and video files across the Internet. Though more than 100 million Internet users experience Real Networks through its ubiquitous media player, the true source of Real Networks's ecosystem potential—and the momentum behind its thriving content ecosystem—is the fact that more than half the audio and video files in use on the Internet are in Real Networks's file format. This content provides the key leverage point for the company's business model and its means of attracting partners. Real Networks is also one of the most effective numbers-based marketing companies in the industry. The company splashes information on its Web site to its customers and the industry at large, from the number of downloads to the hours of audio and video content available in the Real Networks format.

Real Networks has used its content ecosystem to establish the pace of what the company describes as the "business of Internet media." Leveraging its format advantage, Real Networks has rolled out a host of complementary businesses that further entrench the company's format advantage, while creating new business models to help it and its partners create profitable products and services. In anticipating Microsoft's competitive threat, CEO Rob Glaser mapped out a product strategy that would pace the adoption of the company's software and file formats into larger and larger segments of the online audio and video marketplace. In the space of two years, the company's product strategy evolved to include RealJukebox, a program that stores and finds favorite music and video files; Goldpass, a subscription service that provides special access to music and video like CBS's *Big Brother;* and Music-Net, an online music subscription service that uses Real Networks's technology to provide access to the music catalogs of three partners, AOL Time Warner, EMI Group, and Bertelsmann. As its ecosystem grows in scope and the pace of adoption accelerates, Real Networks has been able to hold on to its top ranking versus Microsoft (see figure 4-7). "Real Networks is a dominant force in streaming media," says Jupiter Media Metrix analyst Seamus McAteer. "Don't expect it to roll over."[7]

FIGURE 4 - 7

Real Networks versus Microsoft

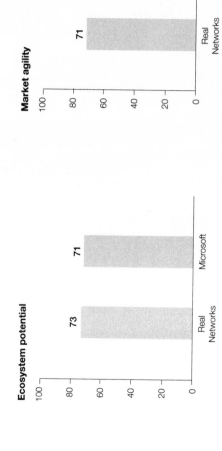

Market Agility and Management Vision

A "sense of urgency" was how Joe Nacchio, the CEO of Qwest and a former high-ranking AT&T executive, described his priorities for the Qwest brand about a year before Qwest announced its merger intentions with U.S. West.[8] (The merger was completed in 1999.) At stake in Nacchio's mind was the future of the telecommunications transition from voice-based communications services to a combined data and voice services business model. Nacchio thought he had two advantages over AT&T, Qwest's largest rival. First, Qwest's optical network was faster and better prepared for transition from voice to a voice and data-services business model. And second, he thought Qwest had better ideas about when and how the business model of the new services world would come to fruition.

Our research into AT&T's market position at that time showed that AT&T's overall brand momentum remained strong relative to competitors, including Qwest, over which it retained a large advantage. But AT&T showed signs of aging (see figure 4-8). Lagging perceptions of the company's market agility and management vision were undermining the sustainability of AT&T's momentum. Nacchio picked up on this competitive weakness and decided Qwest would exploit it.

FIGURE 4 - 8

AT&T's Momentum Profile

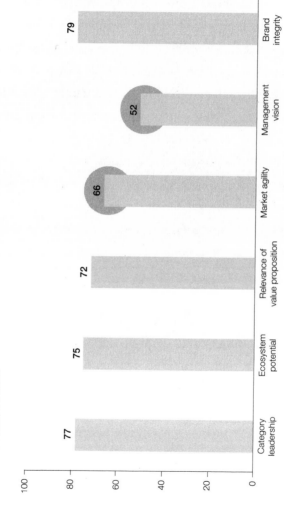

Qwest had yet to build enough of its own brand mass. Nacchio correctly determined that the fastest strategy to build brand momentum was to attack AT&T with a compelling vision of the business future of telecommunications services—followed quickly by a series of partnerships and service strategies aimed at setting the pace for what Nacchio believed would be the keys to winning during the market transition from one business model to another.

"We're moving into a 'bandwidth economy,'" Nacchio told investors at the company's first-ever Wall Street analyst conference.[9] Nacchio explained Qwest's vision for this economy: to be the preeminent provider of applications and services built on top of a new optical- and Internet protocol–based communications network. He also spelled out the company's key milestones for the next year: finishing its network build-out; developing Qwest's ecosystem; and creating new applications and services as the key enablers of the new model for doing business as a telecommunications company. The company backed up its words by forging strategic partnerships with Cisco, Microsoft, and IBM to become the market share leader in enterprise application services. It built CyberCenters around the country to host and manage Internet data centers for large corporations. Qwest established leading indicator customer relationships with companies like General Electric's Medical Systems to develop next-generation strategies for managing medical information. Furthermore, after the merger with U.S. West, Qwest became the largest provider of high-speed Digital Subscriber Line (DSL) technology to consumers in the United States. From the time Nacchio joined Qwest as CEO until mid-2001, Qwest's market capitalization improved by 200 percent, while AT&T's stayed essentially flat.

KEY SUCCESS FACTORS: MARKET AGILITY

- *Understand your lens for pacing customers' expectations:* Know which source of your differentiation is most important to establishing a conceptual framework to guide customers through expectations of change. Examine competitors and identify which sources of their differentiation are waning. Tailor the milestones you want your customers to expect and look for to whatever source or sources of differentiation are the most effective competitive lever. Intel used microprocessor speeds; Oracle used billions of dollars in savings. Don't assume that all milestones are product performance–centric; in some cases, like

Intel's, price-performance thresholds are the only way to envision what the future will hold. But business models, the pace of application adoption, new forms of convenience, and other milestones are equally compelling to customers if they are consistent with your sources of differentiation. Be prepared to take risks with your predictions and outcomes—you won't accumulate market agility if you play it safe.

- *Keep your brand in motion:* Create a road map of product or market milestones to manage customer expectations and provide a basis for advancing the pace of your market space. Stay active with a consistent series of customer and industry announcements against the road map, to reinforce and call attention to the importance of your road map to customer success. Align your road map with a key executive and establish it as his or her key position platform. Intel's Andy Grove was famous for his hands-on demonstrations of next-generation chips at industry events and trade shows—all framed by the Intel product road map.

5

Setting Direction

OF ALL THE WAYS John Chambers evangelized the Internet, four words captured the essence of how he perceived the Internet's potential to change business: "Voice will be free."[1] The idea that the core voice revenues of telephone companies—the very customers on which Cisco was betting its future growth—would eventually dissipate was audacious, and some of Cisco's customers called it arrogant. But the most interesting aspect of Chambers's view of the future was not its ultimate accuracy. What was different about his vision was the fact that it wasn't a vision for Cisco. Chambers was offering a perspective on the future business model of his *customers*.

Until the Marketplace of Ideas, a company's vision typically stayed inside the walls of the organization.

Prior to the widespread adoption of digital technologies like PCs, cell phones, and the Web and the accompanying change in customers' expectations for differentiation, companies used vision predominantly to motivate employees, build morale, and strengthen company culture.

In the 1960s, 1970s, and 1980s, high-profile executives—CEO "rock stars" like Berkshire Hathaway's Warren Buffett, American Airlines's Robert Crandall, Coca-Cola's Roberto Goizueta, HP's Bill Hewlett and David Packard, Chrysler's Lee Iacocca, GE's Reginald Jones and Jack Welch, and IBM's Thomas Watson—reflected their companies' internal focus. These executives were operations wizards, management gurus, sales and marketing geniuses, and investment stars. For their popular management book *Built to Last,* authors James Collins and Jerry Porras of Stanford University studied the leadership practices of companies dating back to the 1930s. Collins and Porras concluded that companies that had communicated a strong sense of purpose to their employees—in the form of an articulated, well-understood vision—and built corresponding business processes were more likely to deliver superior shareholder value over longer periods of time than companies that lacked vision. As role models of this sort of leadership, Collins and Porras identified companies with enduring internal cultures, such as

3M, General Electric, Hewlett-Packard, Merck, Sony, and Walt Disney. By the emergence of the Marketplace of Ideas, what Collins and Porras identified as an important source of competitive advantage inside a company had evolved to become equally important as a differentiator to customers.

This underlying trend was born out of the Marketplace of Products in the early 1980s by a new brand of CEO with a new set of characteristics that reflected the increasingly outward focus of their visions. These CEOs were innovators and technologists whose anti–status quo attitudes and confidence in themselves appropriately challenged people's perceptions of what a CEO should be at a time when the emerging Marketplace of Products challenged perceptions of what a product and a brand should be. Occasionally a few CEOs, such as Steve Jobs at Apple and Philippe Kahn at Borland, emerged as transcendent communicators, able to build credibility by interpreting and positioning the early mainstream digital products for mass audiences.

Through the 1980s and 1990s, two sociocultural factors evolved that would further draw CEOs outside their companies and into the public spotlight. First, the surprising success of mass-market information vehicles such as *USA Today, 60 Minutes,* and even *People* magazine—with their emphasis on personalities, including business leaders—began putting advertising and editorial pressures on traditional business publications such as the *Wall Street Journal, BusinessWeek,* and *Fortune.* Top editors at each of these traditional business publications knew they had to evolve their editorial focus and approach or risk losing their audience to more mainstream media options. At the same time, cable news networks and the Internet, with their capacity for real-time information delivery, were forcing the same traditional business news sources—especially the print publications—to reconsider the depth and breadth of their editorial offerings. Industry personalities and CEOs literally dominated the headlines: One *BusinessWeek* story describing the face-off between Oracle and Microsoft in software was titled "Larry vs. Bill." Furthermore, the rapid growth in spending on digital technologies, both at work and at home, shifted the advertising and, correspondingly, the editorial profile of the popular business media to digital products and services companies. As corporate and personal spending on information technologies increased, these companies evolved to become leading advertisers and the subjects of lead editorial coverage.

The second factor to elevate the CEO to cultural icon status was the new generation of individual investors. With the rapid ascension of personal stockbrokers such as Charles Schwab and E*TRADE, investing moved from the back rooms of financial institutions into the living rooms of most American households. The stock ticker began replacing recent sports events as the lead subject of water cooler and barroom conversations. CEOs became the new stars on CNBC and CNN, establishing an even greater sense of intimacy between business leaders and business and consumer masses.

In summary, the world's capacity for executive visibility—especially for executives of digital companies—grew exponentially and reinforced the demand for executives with presence and a vision of the future. Our momentum research validated the idea that a company's vision of the future could not be limited to its internal audiences. In the same way that the Internet broke down the walls that typically kept a company's information systems at arm's length from its value chain and customers, the Internet also dissolved the barriers between companies and their customers regarding the role of vision in differentiating a brand. In order to achieve momentum, a company has to motivate not just the customers themselves, but also the ecosystem around a customer opportunity. The futures contract that comes with all digital brands must also include the brand extensions in a product or service ecosystem, or the company risks losing a source of differentiation. In addition, the accelerating pace of the digital product model compounds the need to keep these brand extensions aligned with the market opportunity—or risk losing this third-party support to competitors or another category of products.

To address the futures contract he had with Cisco's customers, Chambers had to articulate a vision that promised to move its ecosystem partners in the right direction. In speaking to Cisco's telecommunications customers about the revenue opportunity at stake, Chambers was also trying to rally an entire industry around the economic opportunity available to third parties in the voice-to-data business transition. He had seen IBM and Wang lose ground to more nimble competitors as the business opportunity of corporate computing moved to the PC and computer-server business models, and he was certain that the same inclusive, standards-based business model would prevail for the Internet. "We have no technology religion" is a Cisco mantra to this day, for example. At a strategy level, the company determined that building the new networks required to replace voice revenues with data revenues would transcend Cisco's unique capabilities. The company started using the term "horizontal business model" to describe the evolving ecosystem it envisioned for third parties in this new view of telecommunications. Cisco committed to building this new ecosystem by making fundamental changes to its business strategy. The company, which had relied primarily on direct sales of its products, moved nearly 90 percent of its revenues to a spe-cialized distribution channel. Recognizing that high-end consulting and enterprise software offered valuable channels into the lucrative services market, Cisco made over $1 billion in investments in KPMG and Cap Gemini to build Cisco-specific systems integration and consulting services and signed strategic technology partnerships with IBM, HP, and Oracle, among others. Combined with the other activities Cisco pursued to get at the heart of its customers' business problems—the company's successful Internet Business Solutions Group and its use of Internet applications—Cisco built the sources of differentiation required to generate a compelling sense of direction.

In chapter 2, we defined brand direction as the abil-ity of companies to *anticipate and execute on the inherent market opportunities that come from the impact of technology on markets*. In our momentum model, customers per-ceive brand direction as the combination of man-agement vision and brand integrity. We mentioned previously the role these two forces of digital differen-tiation play in establishing future credibility in the never-ending life cycle of a digital product or service. Speed also plays a role in building future credibility, but it is more an indicator of a company's ability to keep up with the pace of technological change. Direction speaks more pointedly to the factors customers use to judge whether a brand can keep up with the *application* of technology to solve business or personal problems. Customers think, *I know I have options to replace this brand. How much can I trust this company to get it right?* And most of them are also thinking, *Don't just tell me how much I can trust you to solve my most important problems. Show me how you did it yourself so I can learn from you.* As sources of differentiation, management vision and brand integrity provide a framework to manage future credibility into continued customer loyalty during the inevitable transition points that will occur in the underlying technology fabric of the product or service. In our model, brands with management vision have a *well-articulated view of the future,* as well as *visionary leaders* who serve as proselytizers and symbols of the company's vision. Brand integrity refers to how *competent* a company is as a business, how *reputable* the brand is in context to its value proposition, and how the customer perceives how well the brand *lives up to its promises.*

STRATEGY OVERVIEW: MANAGEMENT VISION

Hardware to Software to Thoughtware

We mentioned in chapter 2 that each of the six forces of digital differentiation acts as both a source of differentiation and a channel by which a company's momentum can be communicated. In our experience, CEOs themselves are the most effective channels for communicating management vision as a source of differentiation. One of the unique aspects of the Marketplace of Ideas is the plethora of industry events, trade shows, customer seminars, investment conferences, and press and market analyst vehicles that offer venues for showcasing a CEO and his or her vision. As a result, leveraging a CEO is one of the most cost-effective tools available to companies striving to garner industry and customer attention for a brand's promise of value and to build confidence and future credibility for a brand's differentiators.

Successful digital brands rarely achieve or maintain momentum in the absence of a high-profile CEO. That said, having a high-profile CEO does not guarantee a high degree of momentum; a mass-building product or service strategy is always required. As respected as Eric Schmidt was as Sun's chief technology officer, for example, as CEO of Novell he was unable to translate his personal industry and customer recognition into a product strategy that attracted and accumulated mass. And whereas Steve Jobs reinvigorated the image of Apple's brand and brought renewed energy to Apple as a CEO with international name recognition, the company's market share has not sustained consistent

growth since Jobs rejoined the company in his second
tour of duty as CEO. The lack of mass around Apple's
products continues to be the most important liability in
positioning the Macintosh line of computers as com-
petitively differentiated from its Wintel competitors.

We have found that two intersecting factors influence the likelihood that a CEO's profile with customers will accrue management vision as a source of
differentiation and become a lever, in combination
with other forces of differentiation, for building or
sustaining momentum: category leadership/ecosystem
potential and thought leadership.

MANAGEMENT VISION FACTOR I: THE CEO AND CATEGORY LEADERSHIP/ECOSYSTEM POTENTIAL

The role a product or service plays in solving a problem of personal or business importance puts a CEO's
vision in context. Whereas strength of personality
alone can garner attention over short bursts of time,
the true role of management vision is to sustain accumulated mass throughout the life cycle of a customer
relationship. As a source of future credibility in customers' minds, management vision always exists in relationship to a product or service. Practically speaking,

the potential impact of a CEO's ideas about the future has to align with the role a product or service plays in solving customers' problems. In short, the bigger the promise, the more important the industry role. Consider a pair of recent examples:

- Perhaps no category of digital products or services has had its future credibility scrutinized as much as data storage. While disk drives are considered the ultimate digital commodity, EMC has successfully built a differentiated, relevant position on the other side of the value spectrum. The role EMC CEO Michael Ruettgers established for data storage transcends the undifferentiated nature of disk drives and focuses instead on storage as a value-add information management system for customers. While rivals like IBM compete on the lowest cost per megabyte, EMC has successfully architected a product strategy and built a supporting ecosystem that emphasizes the value of information to customers. As a result, EMC has secured a market share lead over IBM in the large computer system market, where IBM once owned an 85 percent share position. But to maintain its value proposition and the credibility it has built through category leadership and ecosystem potential, EMC is under relentless pressure to stay ahead of the customer doubt that flourishes when cost per megabyte is on a perpetual downward curve. EMC has leveraged Ruettgers as one of its key weapons in maintaining the company's future credibility, cultivating his reputation as a ruthless driver of execution and earning him widespread industry attention and customer recognition. As an example, the *Harvard Business Review* carried an extensive interview with Ruettgers titled "Managing for the Next Big Thing," which detailed EMC's success at anticipating one new technology after another and its ability to consistently build customer value despite the dizzying pace of the category.[2] As the personification of this consistent and meticulous execution—and its importance in sustaining a differentiated position with customers— Ruettgers typifies a momentum-sustaining CEO. And EMC's momentum pays off from a business perspective: By 2002, EMC successfully transitioned about 25 percent of its revenues from hardware systems to higher-margin software that manages the information in its storage systems.

- When Amazon.com first articulated its value proposition for selling books online, founder and CEO Jeff Bezos kept it simple: Convenience

equals customer satisfaction. Bezos's vision was
to build a bookseller that offered the fastest, easi-
est, and most enjoyable shopping experience
possible. As Amazon expanded its service strategy
and content ecosystem to include CDs, videos,
DVDs, toys and games, and electronics, Bezos
worried that Amazon's reputation for customer
service might wane as the company incorporated
the complexity of handling a diverse array of
goods from a greater number of suppliers. Recognizing that promoting or advertising Amazon's successful customer track record (outside of
e-mails posted on the company's Web site) could
be considered arrogant and might set up Amazon
as a target for the same critics who had savaged
the now-defunct e-Toys for missing a large
percentage of its holiday deliveries for Christmas
2000, Bezos settled on a strategy of personalizing
the issue of convenience, taking it on as his own
marketing platform. He began by laying out the
promise of value to customers and put his own
credibility on the line if Amazon failed to ship
customers' Christmas gifts on time, shielding the
company, if necessary. Bezos's personal positioning established a powerful framework for building Amazon's future credibility as the company

expanded beyond books to the "Earth's Biggest Selection." Two years after Amazon extended its content ecosystem, *Business 2.0* writer Eric Nee observed in an article on the state of Amazon's business: "I buy because of the convenience of knowing that what I want is in stock and that I can have it shipped directly to whom I want without worrying that the item will never arrive. And I rest easy knowing that Amazon will solve my problems, should they not arrive. In short, I trust the company."[3]

MANAGEMENT VISION FACTOR 2: THE CEO AND THOUGHT LEADERSHIP

We've said throughout this book that ideas about the impact of technology on business and people's lives are the currency of innovation in the Marketplace of Ideas. Customers expect momentum brands (and their CEOs) to tell them things they don't already know about how to solve old problems in new ways—what we call thought leadership. In a B2B context, thought leaders illustrate over-the-horizon business concepts that describe the impact of digital technologies on a market's business models, business processes, or customer behaviors. "Conceptual innovation" is how the International Thought Leadership Council defines thought leadership.[4] We have found that thought leadership, as an abstract concept, needs to be translated into practical terms for customers. The most effective forms of thought leadership extend beyond the "what" to the "how." In other words, customers want to know more than what to expect; they want to know how to understand the impact of digital technologies on their businesses, and what strategies, approaches, or models to deploy in order to take advantage of the new technologies. For example:

- Tom Siebel of Siebel Systems is the personification of the company's role with customers. Positioned as a salesperson's salesperson, Siebel focuses much of his energy on how to help his customers use CRM (customer relationship management) software to stay ahead of their own marketplace needs. He has written five popular management books, each of which details how Siebel's customers can increasingly leverage software to improve customer satisfaction and loyalty, with ideas about what the future holds, what impact it will have on Siebel's customers, and how customers can take advantage of impending opportunities.

- When John Chambers predicted the future of the telecommunications business model, one of the key elements of his vision was a thought leadership study that estimated the size of the Internet's total impact on the U.S. economy. In partnership with the University of Texas Center for e-Business, Cisco sponsored the Internet Indicators study, which quantified the business impact of the Internet, the growth of Internet-related jobs, the impact of the Internet on overall U.S. economic growth, and the Internet's contribution to the corporate revenue pie. The study illustrated to Cisco's service-provider customers the impending revenue opportunities inherent in their transition to a data-centric business model and identified the important clusters of customer opportunity for service providers to target. Unprecedented in its scope, the study preceded the U.S. government's own study of the Internet Economy by nearly two years, and the data was widely quoted in the business press and financial analyst circles as an example of the economic potential of the Internet. Cisco's Internet Indicators study became the foundation of Chambers's thought leadership platform and contributed greatly to establishing Cisco as a company on the vanguard of shaping the business use of the Internet and the role of networking, as well.

KEY SUCCESS FACTORS: MANAGEMENT VISION

- *Build an executive platform:* Think of your CEO as a product. Position him or her relative to key competitive CEOs and in the context of your product or service strategy. Pinpoint the source of your company's mass and develop a filter that links your CEO's thought leadership to the brand's sources of differentiation. Consider Real Networks's Rob Glaser: While he gets considerable attention as the anti-Microsoft CEO, his personal impact on the audio and video industries and his reputation as a deal maker are the means by which Glaser sustains Real Networks's content ecosystem as its greatest source of differentiation from Microsoft. Encourage your CEO to sacrifice around one of the three key areas of thought leadership: business processes, business models, or customer behavior. (Glaser focuses on business models.) Develop a simple set of rules that reflect the conditions and outcomes of your CEO's view of the future. Look for sources of validation in the academic, consulting, or analyst communities. Market your CEO like a product and build key influencer relationships to contribute to the dialogue and agenda in your product or service category's broader industry. Make clear the significant time commitment required to execute a thought leadership campaign. Put the story into whatever format will keep the CEO consistently focused, but don't become a slave to PowerPoint. Thought leadership is about ideas and future direction, not slides.

- *Keep your CEO grounded:* While personal attention is flattering, the creation of a CEO "rock star" should be viewed as a by-product rather than an objective of investing in a program to develop management vision as a source of differentiation. To offer any value as a proof of future credibility, management vision must be tied inextricably to a product or service strategy. Make sure your CEO's ideas and ambitions are put into the context of product or service strategies. Always try to use your own products to deliver your CEO's executive positioning platform. Package your products into compelling demonstrations where your CEO can showcase your value proposition and sources of mass. Intel's

Andy Grove was famous for demonstrating next-generation processors with next-generation applications from key partners as a way of sharing Intel's product road map. Finally, try to keep your CEO's expectations in perspective. Credible CEOs do not build profiles overnight, and sustainable, serious platforms tied to a company's business model take more time and commitment to propagate than marketing gimmicks.

- *Scale your CEO:* One of the unfortunate consequences of thought leadership in the Marketplace of Ideas is the challenge of communicating exciting, and sometimes complex, ideas about possibilities, new innovations, and new models in a thirty-second television commercial or a one-page ad in the *Wall Street Journal.* As a consequence, the CEO has to be in more places than any schedule could ever accommodate if his or her ideas are to have any business consequence or merit. Develop deliverables that scale your CEO's vision of the future, especially deliverables that are available via the Web. Include video and radio programs to establish a sense of the CEO's personality and how it aligns with the customer experience. The most common and effective channels for thought leadership are public speaking, best practices, case studies, original market research, white papers, and books. These proven tools put your CEO's ideas in decision-making opportunities and conversations—even when he or she isn't in the room. Making these tools available online increases the likelihood of stimulating customer conversations about your product or service; for example, the first chapter in Tom Seibel's latest book is available on his company's Web site.

STRATEGY OVERVIEW: BRAND INTEGRITY

Trust has always been the most subjective of all the factors influencing the quality of a brand's differentiation. In the Marketplace of Ideas, brand integrity captures the very human quality of trust, but marries it with a practical "trust barometer" to gauge a brand's likelihood of continuing to solve a problem of business or personal importance. The role of brand integrity in our research model is to complement management vision in satisfying the trust mind-set of the digital customer and to build future credibility in support of an ongoing customer relationship. The degree of trust people place on brands is always in relation to their problem-solving expectations. As we noted in chapter 2, customers in the Marketplace of Ideas expect more than a paper-based guarantee that something works and will continue to solve problems in the future; they place special value on the companies behind the brands that have leveraged digital products or services themselves to solve problems or gain competitive advantage. The framework for earning the trust of a digital customer and leveraging it as a source of competitive differentiation is built on two key factors: the behaviors of a company and its brand; and the actions, if any, a company takes to demonstrate its successful application and adoption of technology.

Behaviors Are Transparent

In November 1994, Intel discovered a bug inside its Pentium chips that affected certain mathematical computations. By December, the company was inundated with demands that it recall the chip. At first Intel denied that any significant problem existed, but a group of engineers discussing the problem on an Internet forum caught the attention of the trade press and eventually the *New York Times*. After first placing the burden on customers to demonstrate that their Pentium-based PC would produce a mathematical error, Intel eventually agreed to replace all of the chips at a cost of nearly $500 million to the company. Intel's costly mistake and ultimate response highlighted the transparency between people and a company, its products, and its behaviors in the Marketplace of Ideas.

Intel's story demonstrates how the Internet has shortened, if not erased, the line between what happens within the walls of a company and what customers see and experience. As a result, the Internet has elevated the issues of trust and corporate value systems to another level; it provides people with the information they require to determine whether or not the companies they do business with are moving in the direction the companies claim, and whether they possess brand integrity. And—whereas proper and appropriate behaviors are subject to interpretation—trust, fairness, and humility are the dominant characteristics of companies with high brand integrity, as we have found in our research with customers. Companies with high brand integrity make concerted efforts to live up to their promises to customers, do everything in their power to address customers' concerns when problems or issues arise, and demonstrate a consistent lack of hubris in their external communications. Consider this challenging case study on the parameters of brand integrity and the ways in which the transparency created by the broad access to information enabled by the Internet can create liabilities for a brand's momentum.

MICROSOFT AND TRUST, FAIRNESS, AND HUMILITY. Can anything stop Microsoft? In our brand momentum model, Microsoft is the "alpha," or lead, brand. Since we began studying brand positions with digital customers in 1997, Microsoft had consistently been positioned as the role model leader across all six of the forces of digital differentiation—until the end of 1999. That's when customers began to identify and respond to brand integrity as the company's Achilles' heel (see figure 5-1). Whereas the company is well-known in the industry for its hardball competitive tactics, Microsoft's behavior in the United States Department of Justice's antitrust case has called into question the company's brand integrity in the minds of its customers. Three incidents, we believe, contributed to Microsoft's falling trust factor:

- First, in its courtroom defense during the Department of Justice's antitrust hearing exploring Microsoft's alleged monopolistic market practices, Microsoft admitted that a videotaped demonstration of an Internet Explorer–less version of Windows 98—a key piece of evidence in Microsoft's defense against antitrust charges—did not show

FIGURE 5 - 1

Microsoft's Momentum Profile

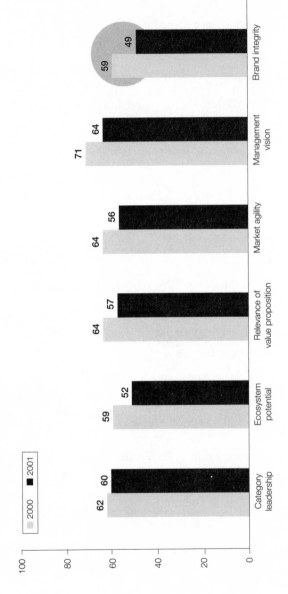

an actual test, but rather a simulation. A second
video omitted a crucial test that was to prove one
of Microsoft's primary claims—that debundling
the Internet Explorer browser from Windows 98
slows the downloading of Web pages.

- Second, in June 1999, a substantial number of Internet users began receiving unsolicited e-mail
from a Microsoft.com address with the subject
heading "Microsoft InSite—Freedom to Innovate." The e-mail implored the recipient to visit
a Web site or call a toll-free hot line to show support for the company in the Department of Justice trial. By mid-July, it was clear the company
had misjudged its audience. As *InfoWorld* editor
Ed Foster wrote in its online edition, "At a moment when the company clearly felt the need for
friends, it seemed instead to be devising brand-
new ways of alienating them."[5] A few weeks
later, on September 16, 1999, Microsoft COO
Robert Herbold sent a letter to the company's
(millions of) shareholders asking them, along
with the firm's 30,000 employees, to "sign up for
the Freedom to Innovate Network by clicking
on [the appropriate Web] link, or by calling our
toll-free number."[6] By January, only 50,000 people had even bothered to visit the site. It was

becoming clear that Microsoft itself could not rally the general public to support its position with the Department of Justice. Finally, in August 2001, the attorneys general of eighteen U.S. states started receiving letters from constituents imploring them to drop their participation in the case to break up Microsoft. Handwritten on personalized stationery, the letters were an impressive show of support for the company and its right to compete freely. But when the letters started arriving from some surprising sources—including a number of people known to be deceased—the effort warranted further investigation. As it turns out, the campaign was an unprecedented effort to give the appearance of a groundswell of support for Microsoft, orchestrated by a political action group, the Americans for Technology Leadership, which was funded by Microsoft. The effort was well documented in an August 2001 *Los Angeles Times* article.[7]

- Finally, in the spring of 2000, Bill Gates and Steve Ballmer appeared in television ads one week after U.S. District Judge Thomas Penfield Jackson ruled that Microsoft had engaged in anticompetitive practices. In the ads, Gates and Ballmer continued the company's chorus of

FIGURE 5 - 2

Microsoft's Brand Integrity

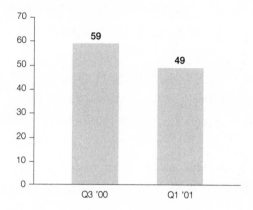

software innovation, promising, "The best is yet to come," while completely ignoring Jackson's ruling, which was clearly top of mind with Microsoft's customers. In doing so, they positioned Microsoft as beyond the reach of the government.

Rather than persuading customers that it had become a more trusted company, Microsoft conveyed a sense of denial, unconcern, and dishonesty regarding the Justice Department's accusations (see figure 5-2). Ironically, the more the company tried to build brand integrity, the more customers recognized the behavior as disingenuous. Microsoft's positioning strategy for these campaigns appeared to be more appropriate for a company competing in a market where only image mattered—something that is not possible in the digital product model. It strongly resembled the Philip Morris campaign, "The People of Philip Morris," which profiles the good deeds of employees at the tobacco company, as a transparent effort to manage perceptions of a company's reputation and history of behavior as if the past did not exist. But as Intel learned with the Pentium, it is tough to hide behind image campaigns when attempting to build future credibility in customers' minds if a product or service is pivotal to solving a problem of business or personal importance. In Microsoft's case, its attempts to control its image have resulted in what many customers have called a "love-hate" relationship with the company.

ACTIONS SPEAK
A BILLION WORDS

About a year after John Chambers decided to become the example to customers looking for answers in deploying Internet-based business applications, Larry Ellison had the same epiphany. Ellison reasoned that the most effective way to position and differentiate the company's new Oracle e-Business suite of applications versus SAP, Siebel, and PeopleSoft was to transform Oracle into an e-business running the very products the company was selling to its customers. For several years Ellison had been touting, "Ten of the ten largest sites on the Internet run Oracle, from Amazon to Yahoo!"[8] But whereas the database portion of Oracle's business was benefiting from the Internet's rise, the applications segment wasn't nearly as dominant. So Ellison committed Oracle to running the company's operations on its own e-Business suite of applications.

Within its first year of deployment, Ellison realized that the cost savings from the applications would be the most effective value proposition for the company's e-Business suite, and the suite's proven track record in saving Oracle money would be its key source of differentiation. In a direct-mail piece to targeted customers, Ellison is quoted as saying, "The question was—once Oracle became an e-business, would our margins improve enough for us to save a billion dollars? The answer turned out to be no. We're going to save a lot more."[9]

What Oracle did was to build the source of differentiation required to establish its brand integrity (see figure 5-3). Emulating what Dell had done in linking its customers and suppliers in a digital network, what Cisco had achieved with e-learning and other applications, and what Schwab had done in digitizing its customer interface, Oracle saw its applications sales jump significantly during the company's 2000 fiscal year.

FIGURE 5 - 3

Brand Integrity: Oracle versus Microsoft

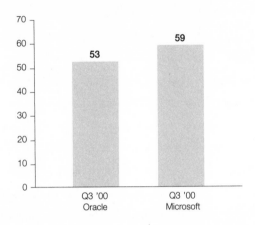

Among the symbols of trust customers look for, few are stronger than achieving the value proposition promised through the internal use of the same digital product or service model being sold to the customers. "You can't sell someone an e-business solution if you're not an e-business yourself," says Sue Bostrom, who runs Cisco's Internet Business Solutions Group.[10] As a source of differentiation, "eating your own dog food," as Cisco describes its internal use of e-applications, isn't as effective for some classes of digital products or services as it is for others. More typically found in B2B applications, this source of differentiation is potent when leveraged in combination with category leadership. The credibility of Dell's value proposition—a better price and better service than Compaq, HP, and IBM—is derived from its category leadership and brand integrity. "We are not a technology company, we are a distribution and services company," says Michael Dell.[11]

KEY SUCCESS FACTORS: BRAND INTEGRITY

- *Make your value system manifest:* Customers' perceptions are built on impressions of the company itself, its role in the industry, and its behavior as a corporate citizen. Make your company's value system known to all employees and external relationships. Embed your company's value system into your customer-facing operations, as well as in your internal behaviors. Be consistent with your metrics of success and establish milestones, such as commitments on lead times, promises of compatibility, and upgrade cycles. Remember that your customers view the company's behavior in the larger world of an ecosystem. Keep your ecosystem aligned on business practices and on product or service issues. Publish errata and bug lists. Finally, don't forget employees. Establish the covenants of the employee relationship and communicate frequently from the CEO on these expectations. A study of companies with an Internet culture found that executive leaders from these companies communicate with their employees at least once a week.

- *Encourage word of mouth among customers:* Brand integrity is built when a customer's perceptions of a brand are borne out by his or her experiences with that brand. These perceptions can be built in a number of ways and are frequently the product of a customer's experience with both a company's brand and its ecosystem. Create opportunities for peer-to-peer conversations—the highest quality impression in the purchase decision process—across your entire ecosystem. Align your CEO's executive positioning platform with your company's metrics of success and leverage the executive platform to encourage word of mouth around your brand's track record. Anticipate customer resistance to and technical difficulties with next-generation products and services and foster open dialogue between the company and customers about their experiences. Sponsor online news groups where customers can go to find help, compare notes with other customers, or just complain.

- *When and if the time comes, be humble:* Customers
  know companies make mistakes. They know
  technology sometimes doesn't work. And they
  know that business leaders are human and therefore fallible. Whatever the circumstances, the
  most respected CEOs make a point of being ac-
  cessible and out in front of issues. "You'll get
  more credit in the good times . . . but more than
  your share of the blame in the bad times," says
  Cisco's Chambers.[12] Great CEOs face the blame
  head on and deal with customer concerns in a
  straightforward manner. The best do it with a
  sense of humility.

CHAPTER 6

Postscript: Momentum, the Dot-Com Bust, and Enronitis

FROM THE TIME WE BEGAN researching this book until it was published, two key events entered the psyche of all digital customers: the dot-com boom-to-bust hype-a-thon and the collapse of public confidence in corporations brought on by the accounting and financial mess of the Enron scandal. Both events served to heighten the relationship between brand integrity and a brand's value proposition, as we've described these forces of differentiation throughout this book. On the one hand, the dot-com bust screams out as a reminder that the most valued market positions are reserved for those products that solve problems of personal or business importance. On the other hand, "Enronitis" challenges every company to revisit and recommit to the ways customers differentiate a trusted brand from others.

On a very simple level, the vast number of Internet pure-plays, or dot-com brands, put too much faith in awareness-building and left little investment for product or service strategies that accumulate genuine market mass around a value proposition, not just brand awareness. Awareness-building was the right strategy for a product that was nothing more than a contrived image, and the purchase process was more typical of an impulse purchase than a considered purchase.

In reality, the notion of an impulse purchase—so prevalent in the Marketplace of Image—is nearly non-existent in the digital product model. Too many factors are involved in building a customer relationship in the digital product model. Consider the difference between buying a $10 package of razor blades and a $10 piece of game software while waiting in the checkout line of Fry's, a popular Silicon Valley electronics superstore. It's a classic impulse purchase situation. The razors can be bought without concern to their applicability; all that matters is that the person waiting in the checkout line sees them, remembers that he or she needs them, and makes the purchase. The software, on the other hand, generates a series of important questions that make a $10 purchase seem like a $500 purchase: What operating systems does it work with? How much memory does it require? Do I have the right software drivers? If the line moves too fast, the unique purchase considerations of the software keep it on the shelf. Or consider the Pets.com buying experience. The invitation to visit Pets.com required a prospect to complete a comprehensive and time-consuming series of actions—from navigating the site to using the virtual shopping basket to submitting confidential credit card and mailing address information to choosing a method of delivery and waiting for the package to arrive. Pets.com asked customers to take on all of this instead of picking up pet supplies at the local pet store—something most pet owners have been doing in exactly the same way for as long as they've had pets. The sum of these new experiences shifted the decision from the comfortable, low-risk realm of impulse purchases to the less cozy, higher-risk, considered purchase realm.

The more important a problem is to solve—and dog food is a very important problem for dog owners—the more considered the purchase is in a digital customer's mind. In our momentum model, an outrageous name, a clever tag line, a puppet, a British butler, or a flashing-light logo—the image attributes of a few dot-com brands—simply do not, in and of themselves, solve people's problems, let alone create a value-based position in people's minds.

There was definitely a little bit of hubris during the dot-com bubble as well. It was simply naïve to assume that consumer habits developed in the 1960s, 1970s, and 1980s would still be in place at the turn of the century. The *Internet Capitalist,* an Internet newsletter from the respected investment banking firm Cowen & Company, chronicled the strategies for success in the dot-com economy. At one time, the *Internet Capitalist* was advocating that dot-com companies spend upwards of 60 percent of their venture capital funding on awareness building to acquire customers (a loosely held idea, in hindsight).

And, of course, the degree of trust ascribed to a brand is the single most important factor in maintaining customer loyalty after a customer is acquired—especially in the digital product model when the product or service purchased is never finished. In this regard, Enronitis exacerbates the expectations for brand integrity in building a momentum-based positioning strategy. In all of our work with companies that sell digital products and services, perhaps few ideas are as coveted as owning the trusted adviser position, especially in B2B market opportunities. As we discussed in chapter 5, the integrity of a brand represents both the behaviors of a company and its brand and the actions, if any, a company takes to demonstrate its successful application and adoption of digital technologies.

We realize that honesty is often characterized as existing in the mind of the beholder, and it's not our place to judge the behaviors of companies as honest or dishonest. We would only suggest that we are in an era of increasing transparency; the likelihood of hiding *any* behavior, questionable or otherwise, has been dramatically reduced by Enron and the government-mandated regulatory changes that will result from the scandal.

But in a momentum-based positioning strategy, the actions a company takes to showcase the application of a digital product or service are also important components of a brand's integrity—and its ability to sustain a value proposition and differentiated position with customers over the course of time. When Cisco announced a $2.2 billion write-down of inventory after the collapse of the Internet bubble in April 2001, the company received this kind of commentary in *BusinessWeek:*

> *Part of the Cisco myth revolved around the company's super-sophisticated information systems. Cisco was supposedly using the Internet to bind together its suppliers and contract manufacturers into a seamless whole, pointing*

*the way to the corporation of the future. In fact, Cisco's
"network organization" did little to soften the impact of
the downturn—or save Cisco from the disastrous inventory buildup.*[1]

Cisco had attached its own successful implementation of Internet applications to its value proposition,
and the inventory write-down chipped away at the integrity of the Cisco brand.

In short, trust is earned, as it always has been; it is
also demonstrated, as it always will be for digital products and services. These are immutable truths about
trust, and the dot-com implosion and the Enron scandal will remind customers of their importance in every
purchase situation, perhaps forever.

In the digital product model, customers, whether
consumers or businesses, who upgrade over and over
and remain loyal to the same brands, say they are satis-
fied with the answers they get to the three questions
that are always on their minds: *Who else is betting on this
company to solve my problems? Is the company moving
quickly enough to keep up? Can I trust it to solve my problems in the future?* In other words, do the product, the
company, and the brand have mass? speed? direction?

Notes

Introduction

1. Michael E. Porter, "What Is Strategy?" *Harvard Business Review,* November–December 1996, 61–78.

Chapter 1

1. Oracle, Annual Report, 1997.
2. Letter to the Editor, *Time,* 14 January 2002, <http://www.time.com/time/covers/1101020114/cover.html>.
3. John Chambers, speech to Cisco's World Wide Analyst Conference (Santa Clara, CA, 4 December 2001).
4. Stewart Alsop, speech to the Agenda Conference (Phoenix, AZ, October 1998).

Chapter 2

1. Andrea Cunningham and Bill Davidow, conversation with Ron Ricci, 1996.
2. John Chambers, speech to Cisco's Strategic Leadership Meeting (May 2000).
3. George Foster, conversation with Ron Ricci, April 2000.

4. Scott Cook, conversation with Ron Ricci, March 1998.

Chapter 3

1. John Chambers, conversation with Ron Ricci, April 1998.

2. Adobe, "Adobe Defines Its Vision for the Third Wave of Publishing" (press release, San Jose, CA, 31 October 2000).

3. Geoffrey Moore, speech to Cisco's Strategic Leadership Meeting (Santa Clara, CA, 15 May 2001).

4. Oracle, Annual Report, 1999.

5. Hassan Fattah, "Casebook No. 55," *Marketing Computers and Technology,* June 2000.

6. Steve Hamm, "Less Ego, More Success," *Business Week,* 23 July 2001, 56.

7. Scott Cook, conversation with Ron Ricci, March 1998.

8. Constance Loizos, "Taking on Autodesk," *Red Herring,* November 1998, <http://www.redherring.com/mag/issue60/autodesk.html>.

9. Steve Hamm, "Less Ego, More Success," 56.

Chapter 4

1. Jim Firestone, conversation with Ron Ricci, May 1998.

2. Steve Rosenbush and Peter Elstrom, "Eight Lessons from the Telecom Mess," *Business Week,* 13 August 2001, <http://www.businessweek.com/magazine/content/01_33/b3745001.htm>.

3. John Chambers, in numerous public statements.

4. John Chambers, conversation with Ron Ricci, November 1998.

5. "Intel Platform Roadmap Update," September 2000, <http://www.one2surf.com/enduser/productlabs/reviews/sept_00/intelplatform/>.

6. John Chambers, speech to Cisco's World Wide Analyst Conference (Santa Clara, CA, 4 December 2001).

7. Jay Greene, Steve Hamm, and Jack Ewing, "Rob Glaser is Racing Upstream," *Business Week,* 3 September 2001, <http://www.businessweek.com/magazine/content/01_36/b3747602.htm>.

8. Joe Nacchio, conversation with Ron Ricci, September 1999.

9. Joe Nacchio, speech to Qwest's Financial Analysts Meeting (New York, NY, July 1998).

Chapter 5

1. John Chambers, in numerous public statements.

2. Michael Ruettgers and Paul Hemp, "Managing for the Next Big Thing: An Interview with EMC's Michael Ruettgers," *Harvard Business Review,* January 2001, 130.

3. Eric Nee, "When Will Jeff Bezos Ever Learn?" *Business 2.0,* 6 July 2000, <http://www.business2.com/articles/web/0,1653,6884,FF.html>.

4. Internet Thought Leadership Council, 1998, <http://www.internationalthought.com/>.

5. Ed Foster, "Don't Look Now, Microsoft Might Be Spamming You," 8 July 1999, <http://www.cnn.com/TECH/computing/9907/08/microsoftspam.idg/>.

6. Declan McCullagh, Politech (Technology in Politics) mailing list archive, Microsoft letter to shareholders, <http://lists.insecure.org/politech/1999/Sep/0025.html>.

7. Joseph Menn and Edmund Sanders, "Lobbyists Tied to Microsoft Wrote Citizens' Letters," *Los Angeles Times,* 23 August 2001.

8. Oracle, advertising campaign, 1999.

9. Sandy Sanderson, Executive Vice President of Oracle, in Oracle direct mail advertising campaign, July 2001.

10. Sue Bostrom, speech to Cisco Partner Summit (Orlando, FL, 1 May 2002).

11. Michael Dell, conversation with Ron Ricci, 1993.

12. John Chambers, conversation with Ron Ricci, April 2001.

Chapter 6

1. "Cisco: Behind the Hype," *BusinessWeek Online*, 21 January 2002, <http://www.businessweek.com/magazine/content/02_03/b3766001.htm>.

Index

Index

About the Authors

Ron Ricci is Vice President of Corporate Positioning at Cisco Systems, Inc., where he is responsible for the strategic positioning of the Cisco brand messages and for helping to maintain Cisco's thought leadership in the Internet economy. He manages Cisco's executive communications function and the Cisco Thought Leadership Network. Ricci's area of expertise is positioning technology companies for market leadership.

Previously, Ricci was a brand positioning consultant and principal at Cunningham Communication, where he worked with companies such as Cisco, IBM, Motorola, Hewlett-Packard, Qwest, and Adobe on their strategic market positions.

Ricci is a member of the board of directors of the Child Abuse Prevention Center, a nonprofit agency that works to prevent child abuse in the San Francisco

Bay Area. He holds a bachelor's degree in politics from Fairfield University in Connecticut and a master's degree in journalism from the University of North Carolina. He lives with his family in Los Gatos, California.

JOHN VOLKMANN is Vice President of Strategic Communications at AMD. His responsibilities include developing worldwide positioning strategies for the company and its key strategic initiatives, including executive thought leadership campaigns.

Prior to joining AMD, Volkmann worked at Citigate Cunningham as the managing director of the positioning group. In this role, he led Cunningham's positioning efforts for industry leaders including Accel Partners, AMD, ADP, @Home Network, Brocade Communications, PeopleSoft, Real Networks, Kodak, Motorola, and Sprint. He has also worked in a brand management capacity with the E&J Gallo Winery on products including Andre and Tott's Sparkling Wine and E&J Brandy.

Volkmann holds a bachelor's degree in mechanical engineering from the University of Wisconsin and an M.B.A. from the Amos Tuck School of Business at Dartmouth College. He lives with his wife and three children in San Mateo, California.